Father's
Message in a Bottle

Loving Letters for Life

Father's
Message in a Bottle

Loving Letters for Life

Edited By: Tyler Hayden

Published by Tyler Hayden,

P.O. Box 1112
Lunenburg, Nova Scotia
Canada
BoJ 2Co

Cover & Page Design: Katherine Marcellino
Copyeditor: Paula Sarson
Printed and bound in USA through Lightning Source

National Library of Canada Cataloguing in Publication

Hayden, Tyler, 1974–

A Father's Message in a Bottle: loving letters for life / Tyler Hayden.

ISBN 978-1-897050-31-6

Self Help. 2. Parenting. 3. Entertainment. I. Title.

I dedicate this book to my Dad and my children.

Dad, there were so many things that needed to happen for our lives to make sense to each other. I cherished our time in your final days — I only wish there could have been more. I will always carry with me your wisdom and love.

For my precious children, I am such a big fan of yours. I am inspired daily by your achievements and caring. I can only hope that you will take advantage of every opportunity you have to live life large and make the most of every moment of every day. I love you so much, and you will always be my princesses.

Dear Father Contributors,

Thank you for your individual contributions to this book. We are so proud to have printed your letters in our first offering of the Message in a Bottle book series. We believe this book will become a shining light in the lives of many adults and children alike. And you each helped achieve this!

It has been a lengthy process getting the book just right with a series in mind. As a result, to help create a sense of continuity for the readers, in some cases we had to make minor adjustments to parts of the book. We took care to ensure the message and meaning of your letters remained intact. We appreciate your understanding as we work toward building a book series that other mothers, fathers, and grandparents can contribute to in a similar manner.

As any child can attest, growing pains are never easy. But the love and support of parents sure make it a little easier. Thanks again.

Sincerely,

Tyler

And as I hung up the phone, it occurred to me,

He'd grown up just like me.

My boy was just like me.

— "Cat's in the Cradle," Harry Chapin, 1974

Message from Tyler

We are so happy you chose to share a *Message In A Bottle*. We are passionate about bringing to the world books like this that help connect people in meaningful ways.

As we move forward in publishing this series of books, we need your help to build a community of people with that same loving and authentic desire to create more meaningful relationships worldwide. We ask you to join us and share our work with your circle of friends and colleagues.

 Like us at: www.facebook.com/messageinabottlebook

 Submit a letter: www.messageinabottlebook.com

 Follow us on Twitter: @mybottlebook

Please share the excitement of connecting with others in meaningful ways through your social and professional networks. We look forward to bringing more messages to more people — and with your help we will make that vision a reality!

Thank you so much for being part of *Message In A Bottle*.

Tyler Hayden
Publisher

Contents

Preface

It seems like a long time ago, a summer much like this one, except I was only a few years older than my eldest daughter Tait is today. I remember sitting by the beach at Camp Wabanaki for closing ceremonies that summer back in 1988. Camp was an amazing experience for me. I raced in the annual canoe challenge and came first in our class. I fell in "summer love" with a girl named Alison. I lived with twelve great guys for four weeks straight; we had the time of our lives. And all those camp experiences, even summer love, pale in comparison to our awesome twelve-day canoeing adventure in the Temagami Wilderness of northern Canada. But somehow, despite all those incredible experiences, standing at closing ceremonies touched my soul the most and I cried.

At age fourteen, I made a life decision. That night by Clear Lake I heard a song called "Cat's in the Cradle" by Harry Chapin. Even then, I recognized the progression of my relationship with my father in the powerful words of that song. I knew that he was always too busy for me. He worked very hard to make ends meet so that my family could have all the "things" we wanted. I understood that my father easily enabled us to have what we wanted, but he did not necessarily supply what we needed.

My life became defined by deciding at that moment in 1988 that I wouldn't be that father. My priorities were clear, family first — everything else second.

Then almost as if I were in a music video for "Cat's in the Cradle," I grew up: earned my license, went to university, and started a family of my own. And I could hear my father saying, "He'd grown up just like me, my boy was just like me." But there was one difference: my wife and daughters come before my career.

I have made what many would consider the "hard choices" when it comes to being a father. I choose to work from home. I work only during the school schedule — no weekends, holidays, or even snow days. Plus, I limit my "touring" to when school is in session. When each of my daughters were born, I made my business a part-time affair and being with them and my wife my full-time commitment. We don't have all the physical "things" we could have if my wife and I put career before family. However, I think we have much, much more with Tait and Breton.

The responsibility of a father is to be active and present with his children and partner, constantly finding ways to connect and reconnect so that his kids know that he loves them and will be there for them, no matter what. Fathers need to build a safety net beneath their children as they grow, giving them the esteem and self-worth that will enable them to succeed in life.

In this book we have had some great fathers grace our pages with their words to their children, messages of hope, love, and even apology. Their hope is to leave a legacy with their children through their words and caring. Our hope is that their words and caring can help you to leave a legacy with your children.

Before you give this book to your child or children, take a few moments and write them a letter, even a few words, in the blank pages we have left for you at the beginning of the book. There is never a bad time to tell your children how important they are to you, and when you do you will open doors of opportunity for them and the generations to follow.

Your Part

A *Father's Message in a Bottle* is meant to be as much a resource about love and caring from other fathers as it is to be one from you. A letter from you will mean so much to your kids. So, we have given you priority seating as the first letter in the book. This will ensure that your letter takes its rightful place as the first thing that your children will read.

To help you write your letter, here are some tips. Sit back and relax. Take some time for yourself and just think about your children. Ponder this question: "If I had twenty minutes of my child's time, what one thing would I want them to remember forever and pass on to their kids?" Take a few moments to jot down some thoughts. Organize those thoughts into a letter. You may wish to begin with a rough draft.

Write from your heart and be as authentic as you can — the love and passion you convey in your letter will mean so much to you children, and their children's children.

How Do You Rebuild Damaged Hearts?

My dear child,

There is no human power that can undo the hurt or the damage. There is no way to go back and relive the past, regain the time lost.

I want you to know only this: my love for you was constant and complete, unconditional and unwavering from the day you were born to this day, and it will remain so as long as I live.

How then, you must ask today — as I know you have asked a thousand times before — could I leave you abandoned, fatherless, while I crawled into a bottle day after day? How can a man choose the cold, fleeting comfort of booze over the warm and tender love of his children? I can't and don't expect you to understand. Indeed, I hope you never do, because only an alcoholic can possibly understand such a thing. The honest truth is this, I made no such choice.

Alcohol was my master. I had no power of choice over it. I say this not as an excuse, but only in the fervent hope you will know there was nothing you could have done, nothing you could change that would have made any difference. You were a child, as perfect and as innocent as any can be.

All fault that needs to find a home rests with me. Alcohol and alcoholism took your father away and robbed you of so much of your childhood that nothing I can do or say now will give it back. I can only ask your forgiveness.

For the sullen and angry man who you could only fear and loathe; for the nights I know you cried yourself to sleep, while you listened to me abuse your mother with ugly words and violent hands; for the promises I made over and over and never kept; for the holidays you woke to excitement but went to bed disappointed; for the accomplishments I didn't share; for the lies I told; and for the lies you told to protect me and protect you from me; for the hole I left in your heart, I can only ask you to look deep into that heart for forgiveness.

There are no apologies. They are too frail and fleeting. You've heard them all before, and you know how hollow they ring.

My battle with booze is over. I no longer fight the life I have. Today, I live it. I didn't make the change. My life changed when I accepted that I was completely powerless over alcohol, and I turned everything over to God. With my life and my will in God's hands, the need to dull life's pains and disappointments left me. In time, so too did the pain.

I can't go back, and you can't go back. What's done is done, and please God, gone. There is today. Indeed, for me there is only today, and the today's that will come. I have no right and no call on any part of your life. I broke that precious gift long ago. But you are my child, and my heart aches to know you. There is an empty place in my soul, a place where you belong.

I know now that love is not a feeling, not merely an emotion. Love is an act. A father's love for his child is not held inside. It must be let free, to nurture, teach, and soothe. You felt none of that love from me. I gave none and can expect none in return. But my love for you was always in my heart, and as I healed it grew to fill my soul.

While I expect nothing, as I have no right to expect anything, I ask for everything. I ask you to look into your heart, to see if there is forgiveness for all I have done and all I have not done as your father. If it is not there to give, I will ask no more. But if it is, is there also a place in your life for your father?

I will wait for your reply . . .

Your father

This letter was submitted anonymously.

Follow the Dream in Your Heart

Dear Brandon and Emma,

Abraham Lincoln said, "In the end, it's not the years in your life that count. It's the life in your years." If you get nothing else out of this writing, I pray that you understand this piece of advice: if you chase a dream your whole life and never reach it, you will be a better person because of the experience and the growth you gain along the way. Too many don't want to risk chasing their dream because they fear being criticized for doing something different. Know that doing anything different will draw criticism; don't let the trivial comments of others define you.

Once a man allows his external environment to shape him, he is forever trying to be all things to all people. If you change your dreams to satisfy another, you forfeit the uniqueness that God gave you. No single person was put on earth to please everyone. When asked what the secret to success is, comedian Bill Cosby said, "I don't know the key to success, but the key to failure is trying to please everybody."

If you are ridiculed for chasing your dream, keep in mind that the critics wish they had your courage, even if they laugh at you. In essence they are trying to minimize your triumphs and bring you down to their level. Don't fall for it; feel sorry for them. Always remember these words by Theodore Roosevelt:

> *The credit belongs to the man who is actually in the arena, whose face is marred by dust and sweat and blood; who strives valiantly; who errs, who comes short again and again, because there is no effort without error and shortcoming; but who does actually strive to do the deeds; who knows great enthusiasms, the great devotions; who spends himself in a worthy cause; who at the best knows in the end the triumph of high achievement, and who at the worst, if he fails, at least fails while daring greatly, so that his place shall never be with*

those cold and timid souls who neither know victory nor defeat.

It is difficult to leave our comfort zones because by nature we seek security. A misconception about security is that the more of it we have, the more freedom and flexibility we enjoy. But people often confuse common thinking with common sense. The most secure people in the world get three square meals a day, a roof over their heads, and all the time they want for recreation and learning. They can be found in state penitentiaries across America. They do have security, but they have no freedom. Run for freedom.

Chasing your dream takes courage, but you were born with all the courage you need. "For God did not give us a spirit of cowardice, but rather a spirit of power and love and self-control" (2 Timothy, 1:7). Understand that courage is not, as Mark Twain essentially said, an absence of fear, but the strength to move forward in spite of fear.

According to John Wayne, courage is being afraid and "saddling up anyway." Chasing your dream also means you'll need to change a few things. Of course it's a risk, but not changing is an even greater risk. If you're not willing to change, you have already reached your maximum potential. You will grow no more.

In the end, the pain of regret is worse than the pain of change. The timeline isn't important. John Barrymore said, "A man is not old until regrets take the place of dreams." Ask anyone who achieved greatness, and they will tell you that it was worth the temporary inconveniences to move to a higher level. Persist, keep forging ahead.

We should not look at who starts the game, and how, but rather who finishes. Paul reflects in the Bible: "I have competed well; I have finished the race; I have kept the faith" (2 Timothy, 4, 7–8). It is my prayer that you can offer similar words when your time on earth is over.

Without question it takes some longer to reach their dreams than others. Calvin Coolidge said of persistence: "Nothing in the world will take the place of persistence. Talent will not; nothing is more common than unsuccessful men with talent. Genius will not; unrewarded genius is almost a proverb. Education will not; the world is full of educated derelicts. Persistence and determination alone are omnipotent. The slogan 'press on' has solved and always will solve the problems of the human race."

Finally, don't be afraid to fail. Without failure there is no means to measure ourselves. It is a necessary part of success. The most dangerous threat to any progress is the belief that failure should be avoided at all costs. Any successful person will tell you that it is impossible to win without setbacks. History is filled with leaders who were willing to look foolish and persist to realize a dream.

Walt Disney went bankrupt in business before becoming successful with his cartoons and theme parks. Looking like a fool to many, Benjamin Franklin flew kites during rainstorms in an attempt to discover electricity; he also became one of our country's first millionaires. Thomas Edison failed thousands of times experimenting to find the right combination for the incandescent light bulb. Through it all, successful people hold the philosophy of "I will until."

I believe that you both have hearts of passion and will fight for those things that stir your souls. You have greatness inside and will impact many people along the way. Now go forth, and claim your dream.

Love,

Dad

Doug Johnson is a college instructor and award-winning humor writer from Colby, KS. His most important role is husband to his wife Melissa and father to their children Brandon and Emma.

Old School Was a Good School

Dear Vance,

Do you ever think about how old I am? I'm asking because when I was young, I always felt my Dad was ancient. You know, of course, how old he was because you and your grandfather had a special relationship. He was old enough to be my grandpa, but he was my father. I sometimes felt like his point of reference about fatherhood was so old, it didn't apply anymore. Heck, when he and your grandma raised your uncles John and Terry, they left home in the fifties. I left home in 1978 . . . slight change of culture!

Funny thing is everything he valued makes so much sense no matter what generation. In fact, I get pretty annoyed with people who think they can reinvent parenting. Some of them have tried, and although there are some exceptions, so many young people today live with a sense of entitlement, selfishness, lack of respect, and arrogance that your grandpa would have been fighting the feeling of smacking 'em.

So, son, I want to leave with you a list of your grandpa's lessons he taught me about raising kids so when you have children (no rush please) you can show them why their grandpa acts like he does.

- Moms come first! Your grandpa had great respect for your grandma, and even though they had real traditional roles, grandpa knew how special she was and treated her that way.

- Kids are not possessions, collectibles, or conversation pieces. They are human beings. Having said that, they are not your equals. Family life is not a democracy. The kids don't get a vote; voice yes, power . . . never!

- Chores are not punishment or a power play! Being a family means contributing to the home, and until you make a living at it, you are not a debater and there will be no discussion. In fact, if you're waiting to be asked, you haven't learned a thing!

- School is a kid's job. It's not the mall, a party, or a hobby you choose. It's also not a democracy. The respect demanded at home will transfer to school. Plus, even if you think you are, you are never, ever, smarter than your teachers. That is their job and they are your superiors.

- When you're not in school, doing homework or chores, you are expected to enjoy your childhood. Laughing, singing, and having fun will be accepted and encouraged . . . always.

- Don't ever get sucked in by the "victim thing"! Bad things happen to good people every day, but too many people use their circumstance as an excuse instead of motivation. No whining allowed.

- Being a parent is also a job, and it's hard work. In fact, next to marriage, it is the toughest job there is, and like life, you get from it what you put in. While we're on the subject, the job is to raise an independent, thoughtful, hard-working, and contributing member of society. It's not a popularity contest.

- You'll always be welcome at home, but at some point you have to leave. Family is where you grow up, and then you start your life. Family will always be there for you, but self-sufficiency should be your goal. Earning success is so much sweeter than getting it handed to you on a silver platter, and you'll be a better person for it.

- One of the principles of golf is to respect the golf gods. So if you're tempted to cheat, lie, or steal, remember the golf gods are always watching!

- No matter how successful you become, never forget where you came from, and always make a point of phoning your parents once a week. You may not have any news worth phoning about, but as much as we're glad you're living your own life, you'll always be our kid. Besides, your mother misses you.

- Never, ever forget that your last name is your family's name and with that comes the responsibility not to disrespect, abuse, or taint it. Everyone's allowed mistakes, but if you're thinking about the golf gods, it shouldn't be an issue.

You know, Vance, the more I write, the more I realize I can continue to add to the list. You're not a dummy. You get the point. Some of the best values our humanity can choose are old and proven. They are also what I feel so blessed to have been given by a great father, a great grandpa . . . a great man who may have been old but has proven to be ageless.

Love,

Dad

Alvin Law was one of Canada's first Thalidomide Babies, the group born with birth defects from the infamous morning-sickness drug. His arms never grew. He was also given up for adoption. However, he was given a home by elderly foster parents who not only taught him to use his feet for hands, but also that he could do anything in life with determination, hard work, and an indomitable spirit. He is a world-class motivational speaker and best-selling author. He can be reached at www.alvinlaw.com. Alvin, wife Darlene, and Vance (along with assorted pets) all live in Calgary, Alberta.

Progress Is a Line through a List

To Duncan, Colin, and Iain,

Many of these things, you have heard from me before, sometimes ad nauseam, but you know the advice comes from the love Mum and I have for you and the hope, as we see you go into the world with a passion for life, that we have been able to give you something to help along the way.

So, prepared like the engineer I am ("progress is a line through a list") and with all the love and hope I have for your future, here is my "Message in a Bottle."

On Goals

Don't waste your life drifting along in the stream. Each of you is a successful rower and knows the effort, commitment, teamwork, and focus it takes to win. Always apply those principles to everything you do:

1. Aim high and believe in that goal. Never waiver.

2. Prepare yourself to achieve your goal. Visualize. Never waiver.

3. Respect those around you that will help you achieve that goal. Never waiver.

4. Listen to your critics only to improve yourself. Most of what you will hear is jealousy. Never waiver.

5. Keep a balance in your life. Work hard / play hard . . . but first work hard.

6. Celebrate hard when you get there. Share the joy.

7. Set your next goal. Never waiver.

Remember, in order to finish something you must first begin. Plan and prepare, "pack your chute" as I have often said, but at some point trust your wits and "jump"!

On Career

People are important in your career. Bosses, peers, subordinates, associates, and customers all have a role to play in your success.

1. Always make yourself more important to the Company than the Company is to you.

2. You will need the help of others to achieve your goals. Remember, leadership is the art of getting someone to do something you want done — because they want to do it.

3. People are motivated by the future.

4. Respect is earned not granted. You earn it by giving respect.

5. Walk like you're going somewhere — always!

6. They say the bigger you are, the harder you fall. This is true, but the climb up is well worth it. You will fail, count on it; but you will also survive. Never let the fear of failure get in the way of your dreams.

On Life

We are not on this planet alone. We have a responsibility to share our gifts and talents with others, and to care about their welfare.

On Family

You are the product of generations of family that hope for your future.

1. Respect that heritage and teach your children the same.

2. Let your kids make mistakes. It's the only way they learn that failure is not a terminal illness.

3. Never buy your child their first car. It is a milestone to independence that they should have all to themselves.

4. When everything around you seems to be dark, there is always family to count on.

On Relationships

Life is a road with many twists and turns . . . for both of you. You need a life partner who will help you hang on in those difficult times and who will count on you for the same.

1. Love with passion. Don't hold back for fear of getting hurt.

2. Choose a partner who makes you laugh, usually at yourself.

3. Marriage is the only partnership where each partner must give more that 50 percent. Be a giver.

4. Marriage is like a garden. It needs tending. Be true to your commitment to each other. When you'd rather strangle them than fix the problem, fix the problem.

5. Share your successes with each other.

On Religion

There are things in the universe that can't be explained. If you want logical explanations for everything, don't hold your breath. Even in science we sometimes use unproven assumptions because the belief in a reasonable assumption proves our theory. In religion it's called "faith." Don't knock it.

Church for the individual, the family, or our society as a whole regardless of denomination or culture, provides Compassion, Community, and Hope to us all. Someday that will be important to you.

Mum and I love you very much and as the next chapter unfolds in your life (and ours) we are as excited as you are about the journey. Give 'er!

Love,

Dad

Angus Beattie, PEng, is a loving father and partner. His business success in construction and design is indisputable. From coast to coast in Canada, you will see the built legacy that has benefitted from Angus's vision. But, more importantly, you need to get ready for the work of his boys — his greatest design and construction project yet!

Thank You

Mes enfants,

There was a time when a tiny baby cried in my arms and looked up to me for comfort. Thank you for teaching me the endlessness of unconditional love.

There was a time when a little girl in a hurry for answers pressed me for guidance. Thank you for teaching me the power of patience.

There was a time when my children's laughter echoed playfully in my soul. Thank you for teaching me to hear with my heart.

There was a time when a young boy desperately craved my knowledge. Thank you for teaching me how to teach you — and how to teach others as well.

There was a time when my children discovered the courage to speak frankly. Thank you for teaching me to listen freely and to act on my imperfections.

There was a time when my children challenged my beliefs — challenged my very way of being. Thank you for teaching me to stand for my values and in so doing, teaching me to stand for you.

There was a time when I was not the father that you would teach me to be. Thank you for making me the man than I am today.

Love,

Dad

Bernard Landreville is one of Quebec's leading professional speakers. He is funny, insightful, and caring — all skills he is thankful to have learned from his children. Find out more about Bernard at www.bernardlandreville.com.

Love Today, Not Tomorrow

My three sons,

You almost died yesterday. On a routine drive through the Taos Canyon to our home, Grandma missed a turn and totalled our car. If not for a barbed wire fence, you would have flipped over and rolled down a bank. The gas tank was ruptured and only because the engine quit, there was no explosion. Lots of shattered glass, twisted metal, and bruised boys. Seat belts and the grace of God saved you.

I was called to the site. I collected you and calmed your fears. I was Dad and I fixed everything, like Dad is supposed to do. Last night at midnight, I lost all vestiges of self-control. As I stared into the darkness, my overactive imagination kicked in.

In my mind, I buried you over and over, just as I had in reality buried my own father two months before. All the details were captured, down to the clothing you were buried in. Jake, you wore your precious soccer shoes. Josh, you had your science books. Cameron, you couldn't sleep for eternity without your stuffed Froggy. Sleep was impossible. So instead, I went downstairs and watched you sleep.

I sat on your beds and talked to each of you, stroking your head and telling you how much you mean to me. I could see you all in my mind's eye.

Jake, your delightfully crooked smile and flashing black eyes. Mister Work Ethic, struggling through fifth grade with tutors and late-night homework. I remembered the pride in your face when you brought home your final report card: four As and four Bs.

Josh, the scientist who aced second grade and was reading at the fifth-grade level. I remembered having to drag you to ski team practice two years ago. This past season, Josh, you and I raced head-to-head in a timed race in front of the entire team and spectators. You beat me by a gate and a half.

Cameron. Irrepressible Cameron, you are the happiest person I have ever known. Three times state snowboard champion, nationally ranked. You are the kid who called me at the office every afternoon during the summer to ask if I could *pleeease* take you golfing. The boy who still thinks his dad is a hero.

I talked to you all. I wondered if my father had come into my room and sat on my bed after one of my near-death experiences. After the time I fell out of our moving car. Or after the time we were night fishing when I fell off the dock and he had to dive in to save me. Or after the time I climbed out of a pickup truck, caught my sleeve in the tailgate, and was dragged blocks before my shirt ripped. Now I can never talk with him again.

I cried. I cried a lot. About what could have been, what I almost lost.

I know I'm a strict father, determined to raise responsible, capable boys to adulthood. Sometimes strictness runs into over-seriousness. Not enough jokes, not enough hugs.

In the words of the famous American philosopher, James Taylor, "Shower the people you love with love. Show them the way that you feel."Now. Not tomorrow. Not next week. Now. I will not be too serious, I will smile more. I will be silly. I will love each of you out loud, not just in my heart.

Love,

Dad

Brinn Colenda is a retired USAF lieutenant colonel. He lives, and skis, with his wife and three sons in the mountains of northern New Mexico.

You Changed the Definition of Success

My dear sons, Liam and James,

All my life I have sought the answer to one question — what does it mean to be supremely successful? I have believed different things at different times in my life. At one point I thought fame was the key to success; if everyone knows and approves of you, surely that's the end goal. Later, I thought being in perfect physical condition — healthy mind and body — were the keys to success; if you had that, I figured, surely there's nothing greater. I even thought that accumulating large, impressive quantities of money was a major part of being successful; after all, money can buy you almost anything, right?

Once the two of you came into this world, at the very instant I met you while the doctors were holding you, I felt myself change inside forever. I remember actually feeling the change. In an instant, I had a new definition of success. It wasn't money. It wasn't physical strength. It wasn't fame. The instant I met the two of you, I felt so much intense love, all I wanted was for the two of you to live a happy life and to have whatever *you* want for your lives. And that is when I finally understood what it really means to be a successful human being — to be genuinely happy and to live the life of your choosing, to have whatever *you* want.

I have dedicated my life — and will continue to dedicate my life with great pleasure — to serving your wonderful mother and to helping you two boys learn how to live a happy life and to get whatever *you* want for yourselves.

I love you both infinitely,

Your father

Brent Finnamore began teaching at University of New Brunswick in the area of human performance and motivation before he even graduated. Today he is a global force in helping people to improve their personal results. He is father to two beautiful young men, Liam and James.

Creating the Happiness Effect

To my very special daughters,

I want to share with you a life lesson that has moved my happiness factor from zero to ten many times: the concept of taking 100 percent responsibility for your life.

You are in your early twenties, and you may have met a lot of people who consider themselves victims of one thing or another. You might even think you are one because you are not where you want to be perhaps due to your parents, your teachers, your relatives, or even your own choices in life. The thing to understand is that everyone is a victim at some point; a good percentage of the folks you talk to have, for one reason or another, felt like a victim of someone else and consequently experienced a lack in life. The individuals who become successful are the ones who don't blame others for their situation, but instead give thanks for all those who helped. When I say successful, I mean happy.

I have found that I am happiest when I am able to be grateful. When I am the most discouraged, sometimes I need to remind myself to be thankful for the fresh air, the birds, nature, others, my health, and usually my spirit is lifted. And when I am most angry or frustrated, I have come to realize that I am either blaming someone else for my situation, or I am not forgiving myself for a stupid choice I made. There is always a consequence, and sometimes it is one you are not prepared for. So best to grin and bear it and say to yourself, I am responsible, and blame no one else and keep yourself moving towards your goal. Visualize what you desire and keep that image playing on your mind's movie screen at all times. Forgive yourself, forgive others, and take control of your life by taking responsibility.

First of all, one is guaranteed an interesting life if one is always seeking truth, caring for oneself, forgiving oneself, and being Respectful of others in their own journeys. Be mindful and careful of those who are on a journey that tempts to lead you away from your heart's desire.

In not listening to your internal voice, you will go wherever chance takes you, and this will teach you some lessons in the area called Cause and Effect. Life is about choices and we are all born with the gift of free will. This is a real blessing but a real danger as well. When making decisions, you must realize that you will never be able to escape the consequences. It takes only an instant to create a heartache that lasts a lifetime, but well-made choices are wonderful contributors to our well-being.

I have learned that I feel most secure and have the greatest peace of mind when I depend on no one else or anything else for my happiness; I hope the same for you. I have learned that our happiness comes internally and not from external things. There is a quote by Chardin that says it all, "we are spiritual beings having a human experience, not human beings having a spiritual experience."

I hope you understand that I feel you are 100 percent responsible for your happiness, and I pray that you get it from seeking truth. Your life will go as far as your character of Trustworthiness will take you; be honest, loyal, and reliable. Be Respectful and follow the Golden Rule. Be Fair and listen to others. Don't blame others. Be considerate of others' feelings. Don't gossip or say ill things of others; before you speak or act, I want you to imagine that what you are about to say or do will be on the front page of the newspaper in the morning, and if it was, how would that make you feel? Be Caring, say thank you, and help others when you can. Most importantly, listen to your small voice, which is God's voice in you trying to guide. Give thanks for your life and all that you have.

I love you so deeply and always will.

Loves,

Dad

Bruce MacNaughton is the owner and creator of the Prince Edward Island Preserve Company and he and Shirley created the Country Gardens of Hope Foundation, New Glasgow Country Gardens and a foundation in support of those suffering from terminal illness. Bruce is a loving father and dynamic professional speaker.

Take Solace, My Son, in God's Promise of Abounding Grace

The hero son,

We recognize heroes as those who persevere in the face of incredible adversity. The hero calls upon great inner strength and character when seemingly insurmountable odds are stacked against him, odds that would prompt others to give in and simply accept fate.

The hero thinks nothing of personal recognition or gain for his actions. We heap platitudes on our heroes and adore them with great accolades. We often lavish them with awards and remember them through ceremony.

My son, you will never receive any recognition or award for the battles you fight, but you are a hero nonetheless. You wake each day to face incredible adversity, yet you continue to summon some power I can't imagine just to survive in a cold world that to you seems frightening and confusing.

You are alone with your fears and anxieties, even when surrounded by people. You have no way to communicate and no one who can answer your questions. If I could, I would remove your pain and help you enjoy life as other boys do. I would watch you grow and develop into a fine man and take your place in the world.

As your father, it brings me to tears to realize that we will likely never engage in normal conversation and never do even the simple things that I always dreamed we would do before you were born. My son, you don't deserve any of this, as none of it comes as a result of your doing. You see, you were born with severe autism. But take solace, as I do, in knowing that through

God's limitless grace when we get to Heaven we will finally speak and have eternity to enjoy each other's company.

Love,

Dad

Major David Kirkland is a very experienced forty-nine-year old military Search and Rescue pilot in a position of leadership. His wife and he have a severely autistic son from whom they have learned what things are important in life. He has gained more knowledge from his son than from all of his other exploits.

If You Don't Get What You Want . . .

My little one,

In Minnesota, they begin displaying the summer toys in April, and when I saw the display of Styrofoam surfboards, I asked my Dad if he would buy me one. He said he would at the end of summer so I'd have it when we rented a lake cabin for a week in late August. I was so excited. I couldn't wait and whenever we went into the store, I'd ask if we could buy the surfboard now. He'd always reply that we'd get it later.

Finally the day came when we could buy the surfboard. I ran down the aisle to the pick one out, but when I got to the spot in the store they were nowhere to be found. School supplies lined the shelves instead. I was heartbroken.

My dad looked me in the eye. "I'm going to tell you what my father told me. One time I found this car I wanted to buy, but I wouldn't have the money until the end of the week. Every day I went by the lot to look at the car, and when the day finally came when I could purchase the car, it was gone. I was so disappointed, and when I told my father, he told me that the reason I didn't get that car was that something better was going to come along. And he was right. A week later, I got a much nicer car for the same amount of money." I smiled weakly. Nothing was going to be better than that surfboard.

I wasn't going to have to wait a week for something better. I was going to have to wait a year. We began walking out of the store when my dad steered me away from the toy aisle to the sporting goods area, and there on the bottom shelf in a cardboard box was a rubber raft.

"Would that raft be better than a surf board?" he asked.

I looked at the picture of the large yellow raft on the outside of the box. The raft looked like it would be big enough for two people. I nodded. The raft was a hundred times better than a

Styrofoam surfboard. That raft supplied fun for a number of summers.

I no longer have the raft, but I do have the advice of my Dad and his father. "If you don't get what you want, it is only because something better is going to come along."

Your dad

Chris Columbus was her father's sixth child and when she was born, he decided they needed a "Chris" in the family. Yes, Chris Columbus is her real name. Chris is an accomplished writer and has shared this great letter of wisdom that has been passed down from her father. Visit her at www.christinecolumbus.net to explore some of her other writings.

A Daughter, a Friend So Bright — If You Could Only Feel How Bright You Shine

My daughter, my friend,

Life somehow confounds the very essence of our reason for who we are. As you grow up, you feel your own pain of who you are and who you struggle to be.

"I have no friends; I don't like anyone at school; I am so alone," you say, wishing that you could find more meaning in your everyday existence. You probably feel everyone talks down about you behind your back. You think about and feel the pain in your loneliness of the teenage years. You wish you could relate to the adults who never cease to tell you what to do.

What you don't hear are the real words of those who care about you. Why? Because we make up our own excuses as to why we are too busy or cannot afford to give you what we think you should have. In so many ways, I want to express to you in tears the joy that I feel for you all the time because I know you love your dad so much, and you have so much to give others.

I shake my head as I tell others how great a mystery you are. You have beaten the odds of growing up in a home full of conflict and weathering the separation of your parents at such a young age. You are one of the best-behaved children I have ever seen, not because you are my daughter. In fact, because of my actions as a parent, I somehow feel you should have become a far more difficult person to be around.

You have been the greatest teacher to me in my lifetime. You taught me to want what I didn't think I was ready for. You gave me a reason to not give up. You gave me the courage to do what I believed in my heart was right, not what others were telling me to do. And yet, you live your life not knowing these things because I was too busy to tell you.

I hope you understand that I left to build you a better world to grow up in. Because the world didn't quite seem ready to give you what you needed. And in my long, never-ending journey, I have felt the light that you shine. I now understand my own reason for being . . . your father. I understand why your godmother called you Ming — the Chinese word for understanding. Because your very existence teaches those around you to understand their own existence. Because your very existence will be to teach understanding and acceptance of ourselves for who we are and what our purpose is.

Your light shines through the fog of conflict and pain; it burns it away, so that only happiness and joy are left. Just as the black sheep in the field may see only white sheep and believe there is no such thing as a black sheep, when you are the brightest light in the room, you may someday know that the light you see in the room comes from you.

You can call me Dad, but I know through what you have taught me that I can call you my friend.

Love,

Dad

> Christopher Hing is a philosophical-minded, free-spirited individual. Although he was born elsewhere, his heart and spirit were born in Montreal. He is a professional speaker, who has embarked on a journey to motivate others to find happiness in this event they experience called life, now, not when they think they will have time to. He is currently creating a workbook and guide to overcoming the obstacles to happiness. Living as a brain transplant specialist, he will with those who open up and want to change their minds.

Leaving . . .

To Jack, Katharine, and Luke,

You left the toothpaste tube uncapped. You left your dishes in your room. You left the car without any gas in the tank. You left dirty shoe tracks across the floor. You left clothes strewn across your bedroom floor. You left good food on your plate. You left the door wide open when it was thirty below. You left your homework until the last minute. You left your chores undone. You left the lights on. You left the freezer door open all night. You left the house without telling me where you were going . . .

You left so much.

But not so much what you left undone, rather you left me with memories, experiences, emotions that are etched in my brain, my heart, my soul.

If things go as a father would hope, I unfortunately will be leaving you one day.

I want you to always know that you left me the greatest gift I could ever imagine — being Dad to you three children and knowing that I am leaving a part of me with you.

With that said, there is nothing else left to say, except, "I love you, I love you, I love you."

I love you,

Dad

David Zinger is the father of three children. David can be found at www.davidzinger.com writing about employee engagement and exploring authentic development and happiness.

Love Always

Dear son,

I cannot begin to tell you how proud I am to have you in my life. Although we don't always see each other, I want you to know I am always here for you. Even though your mother and I went our separate ways years ago, I want you to know it was not because of anything you did. We both love you more than anything in this world. Being with you has brought me so much joy. Even though I had many days of challenges and dark moments, you have always brightened my day and were the light at the end of the tunnel.

Do you remember the time we were driving home one day from the park, and a lot of people were staring at my burn scars? I asked you, "Ryan, are you ok?"

You hesitated and then said, "Dad, I do not understand why people have to stare at you so much." I said to you that people do not mean to stare; they are just a little uncomfortable or curious when people or things look different. Then you replied, "I know Dad, but you're only burned."

That day you really taught me the true meaning of unconditional love and acceptance. You taught me that the scars are not who I am. I am just your dad who will always love you no matter what.

As you know, I was only a teenager when I was burned in a cabin fire. In an instant, my life and many others were changed forever. My young friend, Cory, died in that cabin fire when he was your age all because of a choice we made. We did not listen to the advice from our parents about the dangers of fire because we felt we were careful enough. Although you may not always agree with the advice I try to offer, or it may seem like I don't understand what you're going through, I want you to feel that you can always talk to me about anything.

After spending many years of my life struggling to fit in and following the paths of others, I have finally chosen my own path. Believe me, it hasn't been easy to pick up the pieces of my life from the ashes of that fire, but I have learned that no matter what we go through in life, we are stronger than anything that could ever happen to us. Ryan, I hope you never stop learning, never stop growing, and never stop becoming all you were meant to be. Believe in yourself, and there will be no limit to what you can achieve.

Love always,

Dad

Michael is a burn survivor and motivational speaker who encourages people to choose their own path in life no matter how difficult the road may seem. He spends much of his time in schools talking to youth about the many issues they face today. To reach Michael, visit www.michaelgaultois.ca.

A Dress Code — and Code of Behaviour — for a True Gentleman

To my father's children, grandchildren, and great-grandchildren,

My dad has been my hero.

Tall, strong, good-looking enough for my teenage girlfriends to have crushes on him, he's been the leader, the guide, and the final authority in our family, not that he's perfect. For a long time, he embarrassed us kids on a regular basis.

If we took a date down to the basement rec room and there was a period of prolonged silence, Dad would come to the top of the stairs, flip the light on and off and yell, "I don't hear any Ping-Pong balls!"

Every time we took a shower, he'd bang on the door and shout, "There's nothing you can't get done in there in three minutes!" My dad is a lawyer, and this has been exceedingly cool, but he also fancies himself a doctor, an electrician, and a he-man lumberjack, "worker of the land." As a result, he has been in the emergency room more than Dr. House.

My dad is also a good writer. When he learned that I was going to pursue a writing career, Dad's eyes sparkled as eagerly as my own, and one day, he wrote me the following piece. Enjoy.

> When my wife and I go out in the evening, to a party, a movie, or dinner, I enjoy the company of a short vodka martini while I get ready. My wife thinks my sartorial acumen is dysfunctional and has placed a sign in my dressing area, "Don't Drink and Dress." I pay little attention.

> Having reached almost fourscore in age, I consider most rules outmoded and certainly subject to interpretation. Further, I have my own dress code, which developed in the forties.

Proper dress for a man consists of a blue blazer, oxford cloth button-down, silk rep tie, and gray slacks with loafers. One wears this in fall, winter, and spring. In the summer, a slight change is permitted: a seersucker jacket may be worn in very high temperatures.

My generation mutually accepts such a view. We men who went through the Depression while very young, and then World War II, came home, got a job, got married, had kids — and we all dress up to go out on weekends.

Most of us didn't have much money at the start. But, for a date with girlfriend or wife, for a movie on Saturday night — cost: eighty-five cents each — we dressed up.

Some of us have done well. Some haven't. Either way, if we get together for a reunion, or to reminisce about how much better things used to be, we look like gentlemen. Our wives, now also in their seventies, and still pretty, dress with flair and style and look wonderful.

Recently, some of our friends got together to celebrate someone's birthday. We men in our blazers were handsome. Our ladies were stunning. Sadly, we were surrounded at the restaurant by the younger, "casual" generation, whose idea of true style is to wear blue jeans and leave two or three buttons loose on their shirts. What's wrong with them all? Can't they see that dressing down and dumbing down seem to coincide?

The men of my generation are *not* Neanderthals! We were in the service. We were every race and every religion. We still are.

We apply only this yardstick to friendship: is he a hard worker, does he take care of his family, is he responsible for himself — or does he feel "victimized, polarized, and ostracized."

The younger smart set tends to chuckle at us as a closed-minded group. We *have* closed our minds to certain things.

Pornography on TV, society's unlimited forgiveness of serious felonies, and pervasive personal irresponsibility are among them.

To return to our dress code, probably the main feature of my wardrobe is its age. One blazer I remember buying in 1970 for a wedding. It still looks good, perhaps a tad shiny. And ties that narrow haven't been cut for twenty years. Vest pocket white handkerchiefs are a must, and polished leather dress shoes.

Perhaps the history of our clothes helps to keep us aware and involved in the history of our Country — and we are ill-disposed to relinquish the worthwhile and traditional in either venue.

Love,

Dad, Granddad, and Great-Granddad

James B. Albers is a semi-retired attorney in Columbus, Ohio. Born and raised in Columbus, he and his wife, Louise, have five children, fourteen grandchildren, and two great-grandchildren. His greatest loves are family, friends, and the law. Mr. Albers, who celebrated his eightieth birthday in 2008, also still enjoys tennis, golf, travelling, and writing.

I Love You for Eternity

To my beloved children,

Uncle Mark sent me this email about a message in a bottle from a dad to his kids. You rascals are all grown up, with you Michelle, my *bébé* at twenty-eight, and you Ms. Dawn, my eldest, well at a few years older. I thought long and hard about what message I would really leave in a bottle for you guys.

After a lot of thought and prayer I decided this is what I would share with you, if it were the only thing I could share with you one . . . last time . . . given a tiny little space for a brief message you were to fortuitously find . . . in a bottle. The message would be: I love you!

I have loved each of you from before you were born. I loved you when your mother and I used to talk about the coming of you, long before we were married.

We waited for each of you with enormous excitement and revelled at your arrival. We did our best, and what's left to remember is how much you were loved.

There will never be an accolade I could receive, applause from an audience so thunderous, a recognition or honour bestowed on me so great, and no amount of treasure or fame or worldly recognition could even begin to approach the joy and pleasure I have received from being your dad!

There are many more messages as I am sure you all can imagine; just repeat them to yourselves, you know them! Given the challenge of leaving only one message for the bottle to all my kids, that message would have to be I love you. Always will . . . always have . . . for all eternity!

Love,

Dad

Francis Bologna, USA

You're a Spirit on a Journey

I love you.

Twenty-six years ago you started your journey through life. Wow, what a journey it's been . . . for both of us! I can still see you wrapped up in a blanket, bonnet on your head, when I first saw you. It was love at first sight, or should I say confirmation of a love that was already in my heart.

The early years and the teen years had their ups and downs. Looking back I know that some different decisions on my part might have helped, but as you've taught me, "It's what was supposed to happen, Dad."

Now you're in your mid-twenties and on a growth path that I would never have imagined. School wasn't your best friend, but you have learned more on your own than any teachers could hope to stuff into your head. Keep it going! I learned late that life is a continuous learning journey. It's the continuous learning that keeps us young and vibrant. You know that. The stack of fifteen library books on the table tells me that your focus is intense when the topic strikes your fancy. The recording and planning you're doing with the information you've collected will lead to the content-rich television series you imagine.

At this point, I do have some advice. Fathers are allowed to give advice . . . and sons are allowed to ignore it. My advice is plan well; communicate with those who need to know and follow-up on what you start. All of us dream, many transfer their dreams to reality while others move on to the next dream. I've watched your dreams change. I've seen you go down one path and then see it wasn't the real path for you. Follow your passion! Funny I should use that word because you've probably heard me say that I dislike the word *passion*. It's too intense for my nature and I think it may be too vague for yours. In my terms, do what you like to do. Have fun every day by doing what turns your crank.

51

I give this advice because I see myself in you. Some of the strengths and weaknesses do rub off when you share a home for twenty-six years. Use the tools that are available to help you plan, to keep you on track, and to keep you going to the very end of whatever project you tackle. It's at the end of the journey, when you've done all the follow-up, that you can look back and relish the accomplishment. Think of our recent road trip and the one we took nineteen years ago. We planned the trip, had a great time on the journey, and have the pictures to stimulate our memories. Projects should be like journeys — well planned, shared and enjoyed, and remembered for a lifetime.

You're also on a spiritual journey. Don't let it get in the way of the reality of day-to-day life, and don't let your day-to-day life get in the way of what's in your heart. It's all a balancing act. You are an advanced soul who has to listen to the spirit. Keep it happening for you, and for me. I learn from you every day.

The years with just the two of us in the house have been interesting, challenging, adventurous, and rewarding. May the rest of your life be the same. And, as we've agreed, one day soon I will leave home and go live on that beach in Mexico.

Love,

Dad

Garth Roberts is a motivational speaker and corporate trainer (www.garthroberts.com). He is featured in the movie *The Opus*, and currently divides his time between training frontline leaders and inspiring new writers to follow their dreams.

My Hope Is You Will Consider These . . .

To my daughter,

As a person, and in particular a father, I do not always talk readily and perhaps written word can help with things I do not always say. Fathers and daughters have a special relationship, and despite this certain subjects of conversation do not arise. As a result, I am taking this opportunity to write this special message.

Imparting wisdom to others is difficult enough, but it becomes a greater challenge when it is directed to your own children. It would be grand if wisdom were accepted and applied, but the reality is that in most cases wisdom really does come with age.

I have learned a great deal in my lifetime and hope to continue learning the rest of my life, and I hope the same for you. My greatest hope, however, is that certain values are in place that will serve as a guide on how you conduct your life, and it is this wisdom that I would like to leave with you.

I have discovered it is a lifelong pursuit trying to live a life that has a real purpose and to conduct oneself with a certain expected code. The following points are a basis for how I try to live each day, and I know full well, even after all this time, I still have a long way to go in becoming that person. My hope is that you will consider these and perhaps build on them with your own expectations, as I am certain these will guide you well.

- You may have heard this before, but I believe it has such value that it can bear repeating. Do not be afraid to dream big. Dreams can drive you forward and help make life fulfilling.

- Set goals for yourself.

- Learn from every experience and learn from every person you meet; there is always something to gain that will help you grow. Treat everyone with respect regardless of their actions.

- Believe in the full circle. What you give will return to you in many ways.

- Value friendship; there is no greater gift. Be the best friend that you can be.

- Decide how you would like people to remember or talk about you and become that person in everything you do.

- Become skilled at truly listening.

- Begin each day believing that it will be the best day of your life.

- Surround yourself with positive people.

- Extend a helping hand without waiting to be asked.

- Look for opportunities to do random acts of kindness.

- Try to make differences, even in small ways.

- Learn to understand the true meaning of success.

- Appreciate what life brings you and say thank you with sincerity.

- Be generous.

- Show your loved ones care, respect, and appreciation. Sometimes we treat strangers better than those who are closest to us.

- Appreciate nature and the marvellous world in which we live. Respect all forms of life.

I know that as a father I provided both positive and negative influences for you. It helped to shape who you are, and at the same time you have become your own person. Sometimes the wisdom you display is well beyond your years and I am truly amazed. It is this same wisdom that I know will help you compensate for those influences that could have been better, and that wisdom will also help you to meet my main wish for you, to always have true happiness.

I am proud of who you are and who you have become.

Know that I will always love you and always be with you.

Dad

George Chalmers is a retired executive from one of the top courier companies in the world. He is a loving father who has always worked towards achieving more.

A Father's Commencement Address

My son,

I just can't believe it. As you walked down the aisle last night at graduation and received your diploma, I asked myself, Has it really been almost fourteen years, my son?

It seems like only yesterday when I held you in my arms in the hospital room on the day you were born. You were all wrapped up like a little papoose and your eyes were closed. "He's so beautiful," I remember saying to your mom.

You were born on a Sunday. A wise old German man told me that special children are born on the Lord's Day. We brought you home appropriately on Thanksgiving, and dedicated you to the Lord on Christmas morning.

I remember during the dedication service that Sunday pastor read the story from the book of I Samuel about Hannah and how overjoyed she was when her first-born son Samuel came into the world. She dedicated him to the Lord too, saying: "I also have lent him to the LORD; as long as he lives he shall be lent to the LORD."

Son, there are several things I wish to remind you about now that you are a teenager and will soon embark on your journey through high school. Remember that lots of people are going to try to tell you what to do with your life over the next four years.

Some of those people will have your best interests in mind, and others will not. I want you to cultivate relationships with the first group of people. You might have to make decisions that some of your friends will characterize as "unpopular." It might require you to say "no" to something offered to you. You may even have to end a relationship with someone whom others think is "cool," and they'll try to talk you out of it.

Remember the words of the wise King Solomon: "The righteous should choose his friends carefully, for the way of the wicked leads them astray." I also want you to remember that whatever it is you do, do it enthusiastically — with heart — whether it's something fun like playing soccer or something boring like vacuuming the living room.

When it comes to your studies, I want you to promise that you will be diligent and that you will simply try your best. I want you to be honest always, for honesty is its own reward. And I want you to promise you'll take no shortcuts and you'll do your own work.

While good grades are important, character stands head and shoulders above a numerical average. Out here in the real world, the dishonest and the "shortcutters" usually don't succeed. It's character and hard work that count. Those who have tried to convince us in recent years that character doesn't matter simply don't have a clue what life's all about. Frankly, I don't know how they look at themselves in the mirror or sleep at night.

And to get good grades, you'll need a good night's sleep. I want you to remember what pastor said to you and your classmates during his challenge at commencement last night when he placed a Sacagawea gold dollar into everyone's hand: "Keep this in a special place and let it be a reminder to you of your life, which you are free to spend any way you wish. But you can only spend it once."

And lastly, remember that your mother and I love you and our love will never be conditional on your performance. It will always be unconditional and a result of our relationship with you as your parents.

Congratulations.

Dad

Gregory J. Rummo is a syndicated columnist. His commentaries appear in several New Jersey newspapers. He is the author of two books, *The View from the Grass Roots* and *The View from the Grass Roots — Another Look*. Contact him through his website www.GregRummo.com.

It Comes Full Circle

Dear Kate,

As I sit on the final edge of my fourth decade, about to enter "middle age," I can see that many things in life come full circle.

When I was a baby I was fat and didn't move very fast. Now, even though I hate to admit it, at least one of these has become a permanent state.

When I was young I thought that I could do anything, and I tried to do just that. Now that I am older I know better, but I still try to do anything, as long as I am home by 5 p.m.

When I didn't know better I thought that getting older was not for me and would definitely put a crimp in my style. Now that I am getting older I know for certain that this is actually all true!

When I was younger I wished to be more like my friends, in a smaller family, doing more as a family, travelling more. And now I am proud of my family and our adventures. I realize that this was the path for me and that my family is the grounding I need in my life.

When I was younger I couldn't wait to get older. I wanted to have the mobility, the money, the power to do more things and faster. Now that I have the mobility and the ability, I long to be eighteen again and on a river, thinking of nothing other than what is for dinner that day.

When I was younger I knew that I was invincible. Physically I could do anything I trained for. I had the ability and energy to work without rest for days on end. And mentally I was the eternal optimist. Now, the training takes longer and the results are less impressive, the work needs to be matched with rest, and I worry more. But I'm still invincible!

When I was young I dreamed of meeting the love of my life who would sweep me away into a world without cares and would take care of me. Now, after sixteen years of being with the love of my life, I know that the world is in fact not carefree, and . . . I need more taking care of.

When I was younger I often thought, I won't grow up to be like my Dad — I'll be different: I'll be softer, more present, more this or more that. Now that I have experienced the life of a dad for fourteen years I can see that I am, in fact, more like my dad than I ever imagined. And I treasure those similarities.

Sometimes growing up is about rethinking old beliefs that simply don't serve us well anymore. It's a hard lesson to learn and even harder to act on. Kate, have the courage to act on your beliefs and the wisdom to know that what might be an absolute today also may not be correct tomorrow — and that's okay.

I love you.

Dad

Hugh Culver is a keynote speaker and corporate trainer (www.hughculver.com). Hugh has tackled marathons, mountains, and the Iron man. He belives in powerful choices and thinks that being Kate's Dad is his best choice ever.

Postcards to Joey

Editor's Note: Here is a sampling of postcards that one father wrote. As his job took him on the road internationally, this was a neat way for him to connect and add some little nuggets of love from far off places.

As the years passed he never knew how important those letters were until he sat listening to his daughter give the valedictory address at her High School graduation. She started her speech with this:

"When I was growing up, my dad travelled a lot, but always kept in touch by sending me a postcard from everywhere he went. He didn't just say, "wish you were here" or "miss you", but always sent an inspirational lesson in each card. I would like to share some of those messages with you, the graduating class today."

Then, she would reach into the shoe box, and pick out selected cards one---by---one. She would then read the message on the card, then turn to the class and say: "And this is how each of you, as you go off to find your way in the world, can apply this message". Here are some of those postcards...

Postcard 2

There is a sense of something higher in each of us. So, we all continually strive for greatness, but to achieve greatness, you must first be good. You will find that if being good is too easy, it will be too hard to become great. This is why you should be thankful for all the adversity you experience when you are young, for it is those struggles that will eventually become the fuel for your true achievement.

Postcard 6

You will meet many individuals who love money and use people. Be a person who loves people and uses money. This is one important principle that should be a guide to improving your attitude.

Postcard 14

Achievers do not hide or let emotions deprive them of what they really want. They do first what they fear the most. This way they are able to gain strength by being in control of their emotions. With their goals well established, they live for today. This enables them to maintain their humour and enthusiasm in any crisis they face. Fear is a healthy emotion as long as you are able to manage it and not let it manage you.

Postcard 19

They will not let a life problem cause them to give up. They learn from the experience and create an inner strength from having gone through it. The first principle of leadership you must learn is that you are always moving. If you are not moving others, you are being moved by them. No one in the world is standing still. However, you should not try to control others, nor should you let anyone control you.

Postcard 26

People who are pushy, obnoxious, and blame others are little people with narrow minds. Never allow them to rent any space in your brain. Fill your mind with truth and hope. A positive mental attitude will act as a vaccination and protect you against those who unknowingly try to block or delay you on your journey to self-fulfillment.

Joe was so pleasantly surprised that Joey has chosen to use the postcards he sent. To this day he maintains the tradition with his grandchildren. Now that's legacy.

Joseph Sherren is a world-renowned speaker and consultant at Ethos (www.ethos.ca). Joe is the author of *Vitamin C for a Healthy Workplace*, bestselling author of *iLead* and a member of the Canadian Speaking Hall of Fame. He is a loving dad to three grown children and a loving granddad to two grandchildren.

Crank 'Em Out of the Park

For Madisen, Paige, and Ethan,

I love you all very much! You make every moment of my life better than the last. You all play a great part in my life and without you I wouldn't be who I am today. I am very proud of every one of you and look so forward to spending the rest of our lives being your dad. Words can't describe what you do for me, but know this . . . every breath and every moment I have will always be dedicated to you! I love you all *so* much!

Because I love you so much, I want you to remember a few things that your dad thinks are kinda important.

Do what makes you happy, be flexible, try, learn, and most of all have fun! Just because you can't hit a curveball doesn't mean you can't learn to crank 'em out of the park. Don't just sit there with the bat on your shoulder and do nothing. Learn, ask for help, don't back down, practice, and most of all believe in yourself. Know that you can do it, and do it! You don't have to kill the ball, just make contact and everything will work out. It always does! If you don't take chances you'll never know. And you may never get that chance again.

My grandfather once asked me, "Jonathan, if you live to be a hundred what's fifteen minutes of your life, or a day, or a week, or a month . . . ?" My answer was of course, "Nothing." And he pointed out that's true, but when that fifteen minutes or that week or month are gone, you can never get them back. Don't wait for tomorrow for what you can do today. Give things time and make things happen!

I kind of understood what he was talking about but didn't really appreciate it until later on in life.

A lot of people say, "It is what it is." And yeah, sure, there's a lot of truth in that, but we all have opportunities to make things better and know that we can make a difference. Know that you are only one person, but it only takes one to make all the difference in the world!

Love,

Dad

XOXO

Jonathan Ettinger is a customer service trainer and devoted father. He loves sports and the people in his life. He is happy to return to where he grew up in Digby, Nova Scotia, to raise beautiful children with the love of his life, Cindy.

Thank You for Telling Us

To the strongest person I know,

If you think that having your child kicked out of high school is a difficult life lesson, read on.

When my daughter was almost one, we eased her slowly into a highly recommended daycare centre. Separating from us was definitely not easy. However, as first-time parents, we were assured that the principal had thirty-seven years of experience, and she had "seen everything." Uh-oh.

Two weeks later, we got a call from the principal who asked, "What shall we do about her?" Needless to say, she had her first dropout. Why was our sweet little girl that everyone adored so difficult to care for?

We started to blame ourselves for being "bad" parents. Maybe our daughter was different. The second daycare she went to had a cozier environment. True enough, she did not like it either. She resisted every morning and at times she would not eat or drink at the daycare — not even ice cream or Jell-O. Some parents at the daycare thought that our daughter had a speech impairment or learning disability. She was quiet there and she never said a word the *whole* day. Strange.

Months later, she was still behaving this way. But she would bounce back to life once we picked her up; and then she would eat and chat non-stop and play with us.

We were puzzled and stressed. Dropping her off at daycare was the hardest thing for us to do each day — it was like trying to break her spirit and asking her to conform, to become the "good' child" so that we wouldn't feel bad. We did consider having one of us stay home with her but could not afford the option.

But wasn't our daughter trying to communicate with us through her silence and insubordination at both daycare centres? Once we accepted that, we never stopped reminding her to be herself, no matter how "stubborn" or resistant she seemed to be, and that we love her for who she is, and she must not stop communicating with us, however trying.

Finally after ten months of this struggle, she was accepted into a preschool. Was this going to work out? It did. Our daughter's eyes started to glow again; she played and sang and laughed and was always active and smiling . . . from day one.

She did not have problems saying goodbye to us, and she had fun the whole day! All the staff commented that it seemed our daughter had been there forever. That's what she was trying to tell us: she wanted a different environment — not just daycare.

Despite all the sleepless nights and 24-7 of worrying, we want our daughter to always communicate with us, even through her silence and "insubordination" to authority, to always let us know what she wants and how she feels. We want her to know that we will never break her spirit or ask her to conform to "what everyone else is doing" for the sake of making our lives easier. We want her to know that she taught us to accept ourselves for what we are, and there's always a niche in our lives where we belong. We want her to be true, and to never stop trying. We will always be there to listen to you.

Love,

Dad

Keeping Lau is committed to making a global difference and adventure. He and his family have just begun a new adventure as owners of a English as a Second Language school in beautiful British Columbia, Canada.

Fantastic Teenagers Make Fantastic Men

Dear Spencer and Jacob,

I can't begin to tell you how grateful I am about how you both welcomed me into the family when I proposed to your mother. It's funny — when you were younger, you'd talk about the day we got married as "our wedding." You were as much in our wedding ceremony as we were. It truly was "our wedding," for all four of us.

You've grown into such fantastic young men. People talk about how terrible teenagers are, and I'm so grateful and blessed to have had such wonderful teens as you. You still liked hanging out with the family, you liked going on vacation with us, and you've always had great friends. I'm very proud of the young men you've become.

I'm especially grateful for how lovingly and openly you've accepted your younger brother, Shasta, into our family. Ever since he was born, you've been so excited, and you guys (usually) have lots of fun playing and hanging around with him — and he loves being around you and your friends. You are really good with him and I'm really thankful that he has two role models like you to look up to.

Something else that's been really neat for me is to share my interests with you. You jumped right into some things, like my love of science fiction and fantasy, and you've given me a chance to resuscitate old interests like model rocketry and Dungeons & Dragons. I really appreciate being able to share these things with you, and I value the connection these interests give us.

It's been wonderful to see you each develop your own unique identities. When you were younger, you were often mistaken for twins and almost always did the same things. Now, while you're still each other's best friend and you still share some interests, you're each stepping into who you are as individuals.

Both of you are creative, smart as a whip, and healthy in all ways — you're just finding different channels to express yourselves, which is wonderful.

Spencer, you are such a talented musician and you have an incredible wealth of creativity that you've barely tapped into. You're really growing with the discipline and commitment you're showing to football as well. In everything you do, you have a joy for life and a way of being in the moment that many adults would envy.

Jacob, you have your own creative wellspring that is uniquely yours, and I'm impressed with the time you've invested over the years in your art or being dungeon master for D&D. Your growth in springboard diving is a joy to watch, and it's impressive to see you making progress toward your clear career goals. I'm very impressed by the courage you tapped to change your career path recently — it takes strength to do that.

Thank you both so much for welcoming me into your family, and even though I'm no longer married to your mother, I still see you as my stepsons, and I treasure our relationships. I'm so proud of you. It's a joy to watch you grow.

I love you,

Ravi

Ravi Tangri is the chief rocket scientist at Chrysalis (www.navigatecomplexity.net). He has a background in both nuclear physics and an MBA. He is the loving father to three young men, Spencer, Jacob, and Shasta. Now, if he could only take the helm of the *Enterprise* from Captain Kirk, life would be perfect!

When We Are Together

Hello,

It's been a while. I'm sorry that we haven't talked enough lately.

One day you might be a parent. When you are, you will discover the incredible joy of embracing, caring for, and teaching your child.

Thank you for those wonderful moments you gave me. Some of my best memories are watching you learn to walk, ride your bicycle, and standing at the end of the driveway while waiting for your first school bus ride.

When you were small you would take turns shopping with me. When it was your turn to go grocery shopping with me, I was proud to have you with me. You were well behaved when we went out — not like some of those other children.

I took many photographs of you while you were growing up. I hope that you cherish those photos for the memories they represent.

What did we do together? Hiking, camping, dance class, T-ball, soccer, karate, gymnastics, Cubs, Brownies . . .

I enjoyed driving you, encouraging you, and watching you perform and play. I think of you often and when I dream about you, those are the images that I remember fondly.

So what would I like you to know?

Know that I love you — always have and always will.

And even when we don't show love to each other — I still love you.

Love,

Dad

Editor's Note: I have included this letter from an anonymous dad because I think it speaks to the day-to-day things we as dad's do that really matter. The biggest long-term impacts we make are often at the simple moments we share together like getting groceries, being there for plays and performances, or going for a walk. I think this dad's letter invites children to remember all the "little things" their own dad did that showed he loved them.

So What Went Wrong?

Dear children,

I am not very good with expressing love. I did not learn how to express love. My mother abandoned me when I was three years old. My father raised me. He did many good things for me, for which I am grateful, but expressing love was not one of them.

I married your mother because I believed that we were in love. In hindsight I think that we were both just running away from things. I stubbornly refused to admit that mistake for close to twenty years. Why? I didn't want to do to you what my mother did to me. So I stayed and suffered in silence. Again in hindsight, that was pretty dumb.

As you became teenagers there were bigger issues that we needed to deal with. Unfortunately, your parents were hardly talking to each other. That frustrated me and I fell into my childhood survival pattern; I withdrew. I threw myself into my career and then my new business. Outside of that there was my love of fiction and the solace of drinking. It was not your fault. It was mine. For all of that I am sorry.

There are so many things I wish I could change.

You might wonder why I give you books as gifts every year. Anyone can buy you a sweater or an iPod, but those things don't help you. I try to find books that I think will interest you and stimulate you. If I can't offer you my own insights, then I hope that you will consider the lessons of other thought leaders.

If you are still with me, here are the things I hope that you will learn:

- Ask good questions and listen — even if you don't like the answers. Sometimes you need to ask those difficult questions of yourself.

- Do something that challenges you — often — almost every year.

- Don't label the rest of the world as jerks. Instead marvel at how interesting and strange people can be. Try to understand what motivates them to think differently from you.

- Believe in yourself even though sometimes you will be wrong. That doesn't make you bad, just wrong in that instance. Admit it. Reflect and move on.

- When you don't know what to do, do something. You will discover something that either works or doesn't.

- Make promises in good faith. Later you might need to evaluate them in better faith. Sometimes we make well-intentioned promises, but the circumstances change and we need to re-evaluate our promises. Sometimes doing the right thing is to break that promise.

- Don't let your friends or your family make decisions for you that you should be making for yourself. Consult them — then decide and act on your own.

- If you want to be something, do something. You will only be what you do.

I'm sorry that I wasn't perfect, or even close. You have the opportunity to do better if you choose.

I love you — always have and always will.

Dad

Editor's Note: This is a letter from a brave and loving father I know personally. He asked me to respect his confidentiality. Life is full of tough choices and circumstances. Being a dad is difficult, and this is one fantastic man. I thank him for sharing and helping us to learn from his challenges. I wish for him love and caring.

Fathers Are Flawed and Loving

My dearest Regina,

Life gives us an opportunity to live and belong. It is never perfect, and at times, it can be so unfair. You never chose me for a father, and I never chose you to be my daughter, but you were the result of choices I made, choices made when I was too young to give you all the things you needed and deserved. It took a while, but I now understand the power of our relationship and appreciate you more and more each day.

I often think of the times that we both missed. When I look back I have only glimpses of you growing up. Those too few times we enjoyed together are memories that I cherish and those are the memories that saw me through some very tough times. I have many regrets about not always being there for you. The sadness I feel is only deepened when I think of what you must have gone through. I hope that you can forgive me, for I am truly sorry. My one excuse that I humbly offer is that my own father died so young, long before I was a man and way before you were born. I know he would have loved you and helped me be the father I should have been for you.

You are now a grown woman with a family of your own. You are a beautiful person, more than I could ever have imagined. I may not have been prepared for you when you arrived, but you are the most precious gift I have. I am very glad that I never had the opportunity to choose a daughter; I could never have chosen so well. You are my perfect daughter and a light for me in my not so perfect world. I love you and I love my grandchildren. We have worked hard to repair our relationship, and I am so grateful to be in your life and be called Grandpa by your children.

While others may have their own expectations of us, I only wish for you and me to have the strength to find our own potential. I believe in you and know that you will accomplish great things. Since the day you were born, you have inspired me. Your will to achieve taught me how to overcome all those times I was told "fat chance." I see in you my own whacky sense of humour, but I also see the same front that we put up so that others do not see how we hurt. I just want you to know that I see you for all the wondrous things you are: the good, the silly, the loving, and the stubborn. I see you and love you for all of them. Whatever journey our lives will take going forward, I am asking that we make the choice to be there for each other. We should not let our history be our future. I want no more regrets. No matter what, you are always my daughter and I will always have a special love for you.

Your one and only, flawed and loving and forever,

Dad

From North Carolina and an ex-hostage negotiator, Eric Trogdon now lives in Canada. He is a professional speaker and trainer (www.erictrogdon.com). Regina is his only child.

Love Well Your Children and Your Partner

To my eight children,

Imagine being married to a beautiful wife, fathering eight wonderful children who grew to adulthood, and losing your marriage.

My message is love well.

I loved my wife; I loved my children. Somehow I think I did not love myself. Some might think I loved myself too much. I married the most beautiful woman. We both shared a common cultural heritage. Our parents had emigrated from Scotland and settled down in Prince Edward Island. Our parents were hard working and respected in the community. Everyone supported our love and marriage and our family.

From the beginning of our relationship, my wife and I found ourselves arguing. In retrospect, it is a terrible waste to argue about an issue and never really resolve it. We would argue and never unearth the real cause of the argument. We would get over the argument but never really change. In time that approach to marriage destroyed our relationship.

I loved my children well. I tried to respect the individuality of each of you. I encouraged each of you to work and play to the best of his or her ability and talent. I won and sustained the love from you, my children, into your adulthood.

We did not argue in front of you children, and when we separated you and we hoped the separation would be temporary. We put you in the care of people you knew and loved and that we were confident would support you through our family crisis.

The caregivers cared. I did not, however, love my wife well. I never strayed from her or lost my desire for her. One issue was jealousy. At first, I thought jealousy for my wife was flattering; however, suspicion and criticism of the one you love is destructive. Because she was beautiful and friendly to other males, I always feared I would lose her to someone else. The fault lay with me, not with my wife. She swore that she never flirted or strayed from me.

There was another issue that may have been more important than I wanted to admit. I often socialized in the community with brothers and friends by spending time at the pub and then appearing at the doorstep late at night looking for my wife to set up a lunch for everyone. Years ago, when I was not bringing in much money, this request put an embarrassing burden on her. With eight children in hard times, it was not easy to feed a group of loud, drunken card players, but I insisted she do so. She valued hospitality, but I regularly put her in an impossible position before family and neighbours.

After too many years of my arrogant and destructive attitude, she had had enough. Almost unheard of in the community at the time, we separated and never restored our marriage. We cooperated in finding family members who would take each one of you children into their homes.

Before we parted, my wife tried to help me understand that it was not the jealousy that hurt. Rather, it was the habitual distrust and disrespect that ate away at our marriage. The greatest pain came from her realization that after twenty years, I still had no understanding of her character or her worth. By the time she died a very few years after our separation, I could see how much you children had loved your mother, and that love never waned.

Luckily, I still felt loved by my children. At the end of my life, I am facing my responsibility in not loving well. I criticized my wife, yet I was the one who was feeling vulnerable, inadequate, undeserving. I did not feel happy about my work throughout the years of our marriage.

Despite living in a farming and fishing community, I could not farm well neither could I fish well. I was good at carpentry, but there was little money in the trade years ago. I worked as a lighthouse keeper for a few years. The isolation and low pay were discouraging. I used to complain about my work. I never sought the understanding that would help me focus on making myself happier. Instead I took my personal unhappiness out on a wonderful woman and lost her.

Dad

Having taught high school students how to read and write for many years, John Dunphy is writing a collection of short stories focused on two families, immigrants from Scotland and Ireland, who establish new roots in the Maritimes. The stories cover events from settlement times to the present.

Cherish the People in Your Life

To Courtney, Ivan, and my future children,

Over the course of my life I continually find myself searching for the answer to what is wrong with this world. This list continues to grow by the minute. Children seem to be less and less obedient to their parents, wealth seems to be less distributed amongst the people, government continues to fail the people, society seems to be falling apart, and the institution of marriage or commitment holds little value in today's relationships.

Although it is easy to cite many problems, it is very difficult to find any viable solutions. If I had the power to fix the world I would erase the word *greed* from our vocabularies and minds; however, this is not possible.

Realistically, neither you nor I can change the world, so don't try to save it. Instead, embrace what you can control, your own actions and decisions.

I ask that you attempt to avoid greed in your own life. I am not suggesting that you donate all of your time and money to charity, but more that you attempt to consider the well-being of everyone affected by the decisions you make. The choices you make will impact many people, often the ones you care most about.

Cherish these people, especially the friendships you establish along your path in life. By respecting these relationships you will always have core strength to rely on when you need it most.

My life has never been easy, but the things I am most grateful for are the friendships I have made along the way.

Sincerely,

Dad

Mark Landry works in the IT field. He has walked a jagged path. With every twist and turn he learns and creates great results. Mark finds love and respect with friends and family. And in those relationships he finds his true wealth and happiness.

First Poem for a Child

This is a broken down leaf,

This is a salty sidewalk,

These are absurd cars.

These are the cruel laws and the machinations of man.

You will discern each and each their wickedness and what is engendered in thin paper constitutions.

All of this you will learn in due time,

In your own sweet time, son, daughter of mine.

These are fickle words sometimes disguised as poetry,

Sometimes as truth.

There are other truths and other lies more volatile yet to come,

Be ready and forewarned, sweet child of mine.

But for now, enjoy this new journey called life.

Be comforted by the fact that you are now shielded in your womb home.

Long may you live there.

In due time, in your own sweet time, daughter, son of mine, you will come to know the machinations of mankind.

Denis Robillard is married. He was born and raised in Northern Ontario on blueberries and walleye. To date he has been a historical interpreter, body guard, probation officer, and journalist. He presently works as an English teacher in Windsor, Ontario. Robillard has more than eighty publications to date. Poems, stories, and articles have appeared in magazines, journals, and books in Canada, England, and the United States.

Take Your Own Advice

Dear Tara, Courtney, and Dustin,

When I was just starting out as an advertising copywriter, I did what every aspiring copywriter or creative artist has to do. I remember building a portfolio of mock ads that I made up for imaginary products and modifying existing ads that I had found in magazines.

The next thing an aspiring copywriter does is shop his or her portfolio around, and again, that's what I did. I found the addresses of the biggest advertising agencies in the city and I got the names of the creative directors. Then I sent them all letters telling them about me and all the wonderful things I could do for them. For some of them, I also went around personally to drop off a gimmick — a full-size fake arm that I bought at the local novelty store. On the sleeve in big letters, I wrote this headline, "'Free hand. Brain extra." Underneath I put my name and phone number.

Then I waited a few days and summoned up the courage to call them. The letters worked, and the gimmick worked even better. I got a lot of interviews.

So here I was, fresh out of school, full of excitement about how I was going to change the world. I bet you feel the same way as you prepare to start your own careers.

It was intimidating to walk into major advertising agencies with their awards posted all over the walls of their reception areas. It was even more intimidating to maintain my self-confidence in the interviews as these big, important creative directors with even bigger egos flipped through the pages of my pitiful amateur portfolio.

I remember their reactions — even the expressions on their faces — as they quickly passed over some pages and stopped to look a little harder on other pages. Inevitably, they'd say to me,

"This ad doesn't do your portfolio justice — you should take it out. But this ad is brilliant. It works. I like it. Well done."

Every time I opened up my book for another creative director, I received that comment. The only problem was every creative director picked a different ad for which one was bad and which one was brilliant.

And so I quickly learned that no matter how experienced they were, how famous, how smart, how many awards they won or how much conviction they spoke with, I was the one who had to figure out what worked and what didn't, what was good and what was bad, and why.

Yes, listen to everyone's advice, but take only your own.

Love,

Dad

Michel Neray has changed the world after all. He created the world's first online searchable directory of creative professionals and is a pioneer in the area of core messaging. His company, The Essential Message (www.essentialmessage.com), helps companies and individuals discover their true differentiation and then communicate it in the most compelling way. Together with his wife Barbara, he also takes some credit for raising the most wonderful kids any parent can ask for.

Appreciate What You Have

Dear Jennifer, Jeff, and Jason,

I met a colleague at a local association meeting. He was a quiet, unassuming person. Over the next few years we reconnected on a number of occasions, but I never really made an effort to get to know him better.

One day, out of the blue, he called. He had been diagnosed with an aggressive form of cancer. He wanted to transfer his material to audio before passing, and he asked for my help. We quickly put a plan together and he began his task.

As we progressed, I became aware of his uniqueness and incredible value. I desperately wanted to get to know him better. But there simply wasn't time. Within a few weeks he was gone. To this day, I regret my earlier missed opportunities.

If I had only one thought I could share, one simple statement to pass along about lessons learned, I would tell you this one thing: appreciate what you have. And put this into a different context than the material things we focus on when this is usually mentioned.

Society has done an outstanding job of showcasing the many riches it has to offer. In striving to get more, do more, and be more, we all too often overlook the treasures we have at hand. It's so easy to lose perspective about what's really important.

What's most important has more to do with the people we meet and the people we know than how much we have or how high we rise. You're living proof of that. As I watch how you've grown and learned and lived, I'm acutely conscious of how much I missed in my quest for the Holy Grail. So here's my message. Look around you. Look closely. Look deeply. Invest in the richness of the people around you, whether they are family, friends, or colleagues. Here is your greatest gift, your most powerful asset.

So put up with your family's shortcomings, they are your heritage. Support your friends, and they will support you in times of need. Invest in making connections; these new contacts will open new worlds. But above all, take time every day to reflect on those around you and appreciate them.

Tomorrow may be too late.

Dad

Michael Hughes is known as Canada's networking guru (www.NetworkingForResults.com), but more importantly, he is dad to three wonderful children: Jennifer, Jeff, and Jason.

A Father's Dream for His Unborn Child

My dearest little one,

I write this letter to you, my soon to be son or daughter, from my company's international headquarters in Panama. I am now realizing that I am living my dream of international business by "marketing the world to the world." My dream is a reality, and I now look forward to assisting you in realizing your dreams.

I have been fortunate to be raised by two wonderful parents. I lived my childhood on a farm in the Prairies, where a strong work ethic was instilled into me. With that, as well as my parents' loving guidance and the beautiful rural setting, I felt I was set up for success from the beginning.

I would not trade my childhood for the world. What I learnt from this I use daily in my family life and business life. I was taught to always treat others with respect and listen while other people were talking. Those two skills now assist me with our team approach to business and openness to new ideas.

I have also learnt that taking risks is okay and part of the journey to success. You see, being raised on a farm our entire livelihood was based on risk and we learnt to manage that risk.

To this day, if I make a mistake in business I always ensure I use it as a learning experience. You will skin your knees; I will be there to help you pick yourself up and encourage you to move forward.

I only hope that I am able to provide a similar upbringing for you as I received.

I have had the great fortune to meet a wonderful lady, your mother, and through our love we have made you. Your mom and I have travelled the globe together, experiencing different cultures and meeting fascinating people. We are so excited to welcome you into this world and look forward to continuing this journey together with you.

Your dad

Michael Burnay is vice-president of International Sales Properties International Marketing Group Inc. Mike grew up in rural Saskatchewan, cultivating hundreds of acres to feed the world. Today, Mike takes that same love for cultivation and is growing a successful business that places family first.

Above All, Be True to Yourself

Dear Lauren and Jeff,

The message in my bottle comes from a life filled with adventure. I've always wanted to know what's around the next curve, to see how things are done in different parts of the world, and to experience as much as I can of what life offers. To the extent that I was able to do these things, and to share them with my children, I feel blessed and honoured to be able to look back and perhaps attempt to identify a few of the sights, sounds, and experiences that have stayed with me these years.

Forty years of travel have shown me that people everywhere are basically good and not very different. They all are trying to live as well as possible, to protect and provide for their families, and to find what enjoyment they can in their daily lives. To this end I can only pass along words I first heard from a high school teacher (although she paraphrased it from another slightly better known English teacher), "Be true to yourself," spend time establishing your values, and let them guide your decisions in life.

To the extent possible, I would advise anyone to not be shy about dreaming, travelling, and experiencing life to the fullest. Remember it's not how long you live that matters, but how alive you are as you live.

So make every day count, and treat every experience as an adventure. Above all, "Be true to yourself."

Love,

Dad

Gerry Sokolik is a retired pilot and property investor from Spokane, Washington. He flew for the US Air Force as well as commercial airlines. Gerry loves his kids and grandkids and wants them to be successful and to see the world and all its beauty. When Gerry is not on an adventure, you'll find him riding his motorbike through the backwoods of Newfoundland, Canada.

Sometimes Dads Learn Too

Dear Daughter,

Not long ago I came to the conclusion that you were simply an "untidy person," and I told you so, in a fit of frustration, after helping you find a needed lost item under a heap of mess. Because you had seemingly proven yourself consistently unable to conform to even the most basic tidiness required by your mom and I, the response seemed natural and fair, an explanation of the facts. To me it was incomprehensible that you didn't make the effort to keep your room tidy and play your part in avoiding the inevitable daily conflict. Then something occurred to me.

I thought to myself, my daughter's mother and I had separated when she was very young. I know that her mother had developed the habit of tidying up after her. The child had soon learned that garments, shoes, and towels discarded on the floor would miraculously end up back in her closet neatly folded, often washed and ironed, too. No one had ever shown her how to tidy her room. It was little wonder the child had no concept of why it was necessary to tidy up after herself! It hadn't been necessary so far; she had a service to do it for her. (At least at one of her residences!)

So one day, instead of confining you to your room until it was tidy, I invested some time showing you exactly what was expected. We picked up things together; we put them back where they lived so they could easily be found again. We both folded your clothes — together. You were taught that day, and I was sure you understood very clearly, that by being tidy you created more space to pack your things. Things wouldn't go missing so easily. You then rediscovered things that had been missing for months, including six pairs of school socks and a favourite charm. You were able to discard items that were too small for you or no longer needed. Now we could all look forward to a tidy room, a great attitude, and no more conflict — what a relief!

No such luck. Within three days it was back to being a frightful mess. "Sorry Dad. Guess I'm just an untidy person," you shrugged cheerfully. I stared in disbelief. I teach people communication skills, yet somehow, I was making little headway here. I hoped that I'd laid some manner of foundation, but clearly the house was by no means built yet.

A few days later, while chatting to a friend, the subject of your untidiness surfaced. My friend then asked, "Have you actually told her that she is an untidy person?"

"Yes, using those very words," I replied.

"Well then, she's simply living up to your expectation of her, isn't she?"

It hit me like a bolt between the eyes. I had provided just the excuse you needed, and you were living up to that label. A human who commits a crime is assigned the label "criminal." It doesn't take long for that person to adjust to his/her new station in life. Just so, you had settled comfortably into being the untidy person that you were now labelled. Every time you tidied up your room, the label no longer fit, so you had "permission" to allow the room to return to its default state — untidy. Why? Well you're just an untidy person, after all!

The following day, I walked into your room. The room itself was in quite a mess, but your clothes cupboard was still quite tidy. I commented, "I can see you're really making an effort with your clothes cupboard. Well done!" Ignoring the state of the rest of the room, I walked out.

The next day in the car, on the way back from school, I said to you, "I have an apology to make to you. A few weeks ago I called you an untidy person. That was very wrong of me. What I am seeing now is that you are really a tidy person who sometimes has an 'off day.' Maybe there are times when I've walked into your room that you're still busy and had been planning to tackle it later. I have also noticed how you are really trying to keep your cupboards tidy." You beamed at me.

Your room still degenerates into a mess, quite often, actually. We've talked about it and you have indicated that there are times when you're busy, and that you can live with it for a while. You understand, though, that your while and mine are of considerably different durations. So we now have an agreement. Twice a week, on vacuuming day, you make sure that the room is in a fit state to be cleaned. You are no longer "an untidy person." And I've learned to be mindful before labelling someone I care about, even if it was done subconsciously.

I've discovered that one of the greatest gifts we can give to those we love is the confirmation that they are okay, and that they don't have to live up to all of our expectations all the time to be okay. They're okay, simply because they are. I'm grateful that you had the patience to teach me some of the lessons that I've needed to learn.

Thank you. I love you.

Dad

Paul du Toit is a certified professional speaker from South Africa (www.pauldutoit.net). Paul specializes in helping people communicate ideas and shift their mindset in the area of presentation, client service, and possibility.

The Explorer

My boys,

As a father, there is so much I want to tell you. There are things I've learned and wisdom that I want to pass along to you as soon as I can. And, over time, I hope I will have the courage to be able to tell you how much I don't know and how much I wish I had more patience and more wisdom to help you through life.

Because I care so deeply for you three boys, I can be overwhelmed with how much there is to tell you and the responsibilities related to being a good parent to you, how much there is that I want to share with you. And, over time, I will hopefully be given the chance to share, teach, and learn with you.

One of the things I now know is a truth is how powerful you each are already as kids. What you can do right now is truly incredible at such young ages. And, within this truth lies one powerful message for you boys, for me, and for all of us — the inexplicable power of what we are capable of at any age.

When we are young, we are definitely able to play and to explore in ways unlike any other time in our lives. I hope that you will always be explorers and full of play. These traits allow people to go through life with happiness, success, and contentment. I believe that these traits as much as any other will help you lead the lives you were meant to live.

We are so fortunate to have the whole planet available to us. We can explore and discover the treasures that it has to offer, and hopefully as you boys make your discoveries, you will share these with others and with your dad.

Most importantly, I hope that you don't wait. I hope that you don't wait until tomorrow. I hope that you don't wait until you "grow up" to go and try something. I hope that you don't wait until you think you are smart enough, experienced enough, rich

90

enough, or comfortable enough to go forward and start that new exploration or project.

Go forward my little explorers and discover the mountains and the valleys, the rivers and the seas, the flora and the fauna, the new and the familiar, and most importantly, your schemes and your dreams.

Love,

Dad

Paul Frazer is a professional speaker, consultant, author, and explorer. His company, Mindscape, is dedicated to helping individuals and organizations become simply world-class by creating the perfect tools, strategies, and mindset for success. A former IT consultant and executive, Paul has conquered marathons, triathlons, and Mount Kilimanjaro, and has lived and worked overseas. As an engineer, Paul has an insatiable curiosity about how things work, particularly the fascinating terrain of the mind.

Perfectionism, the Cure for Happiness

Dear Greg,

It's time that I really told you how special and important you are to me. You've achieved a lot despite having to make sacrifices that were important to our family.

We've lived through much together, the ups and downs of everyday life. We've played, laughed, cried, celebrated, and grieved together. These things have served to bring us closer together and they are a testament to the belief that relationships are built through shared experiences.

I know there have been times, maybe even months and years, that you thought I wasn't proud of you, but that was never so. I am also painfully aware of how difficult it can be to grow up with a perfectionist father. Yet you've done so, and very well I might add.

As with any good twelve-step program, the first step is to admit that you have a problem. It was Clayton Lafferty, PhD, who said to me, "Perfectionism is the sure cure for happiness." At the time I thought that he was kidding, but he was speaking directly to me.

I'd love to say that the past is the past but the truth is, how we see the world is filtered through the life experiences we have. As a recovering perfectionist, I have learned that the past is not our future.

Remember the time you took a day off, without pay, to drive from Toronto to Montreal to deliver a parcel to me? That truly was a very special day, wherein I learned that selfless acts like yours is what love is all about.

It's time that you and I embraced a new future, one filled with joy and happiness. Let's go do something that a perfectionist wouldn't do and put on a couple of goofy hats and go out for a beer. Maybe we could wear those goofy hats until the Toronto Maple Leafs win the Stanley Cup!

On second thought, maybe we should just settle for wearing the hats when we take your mother out for dinner.

See you Sunday.

Lots of love,

Dad

Sid Ridgley, CSP, MBA, is a recovering perfectionist who assists leaders in building great places to work and to do business with. Through keynotes, seminars, consulting, and a host of diagnostic tools, he helps people get past the details by focusing on results.

Do-do Magnets Be Gone

To my children,

There are people who love problems. These people have many names. My favourite is do-do magnets. They're addicted to troubles. They find problematic issues irresistible and share their woes with everyone within earshot. Sure, it's natural to turn your attention on something going wrong. But fixating on the problem is not the solution.

There are three kinds of problems with their own set of solutions.

1. Circumstantial problems.

> Get past these kinds of problems as soon as you can. Examples would be getting double-booked, finding the right kind of spaghetti sauce, a bad shoe/purse combination, or a rip in your pants just seconds before a speech.

> The answer is simple. Look past the problem and immediately focus on the solution. Don't be an a.k.a. Poop Attractor. It's a problem. Get over it. Leave it behind and march directly towards a resolution. (And face the crowd without turning to see the PowerPoint slide!)

2. Fear-based problems.

> In situations that cause anxiety, take a page out of a flight attendant's takeoff guide. "In case of depressurization, oxygen masks will drop down from the overhead bins. Place the plastic cup over your nose and mouth and," get this, "breathe normally."

> Breathe normally?

> *Breathe normally?*

We are plummeting towards the earth at hundreds of kilometres per hour. Who's planning on breathing normally?

Seriously, most fears are about things that haven't happened: my teenager missed her curfew and she hasn't checked in; I messed up at work and my boss doesn't know yet; the car is making a funny noise and I bet it's the transmission going out; oh, that hole in the ozone layer is just a fad. . . . (But some fears are worth paying attention to.)

Obsessing over the problem is only going to hinder clear thinking. Leave that up to the "Big Boom Boom Hold-er On-er" who likes to obsess about problems. With fear-based problems the smartest, most efficient thing you can do is immediately plan a way towards your targeted result. Then take action!

3. Pain-based problems

Pain-based problems are the worst. Pain-based problems are a huge distraction, especially when there is a "Look-Who-Done-Me-Wrong Ka Ka Cowboy" in our midst. We don't need him to remind us of the financial pressures, relationship woes, employment issues, or health problems that crop up now and then. Yet pain-based problems need to be addressed immediately. I recommend the following.

- Acknowledge the problem. Ignoring the problem is like stuffing it into a drawer and pretending it doesn't exist. It is human nature to avoid a problem. It is also human nature to solve problems. Acknowledge the problem and be honest with yourself and others that the problem exists.

- Isolate the problem. Isolate the issue and you accelerate a solution. Alcoholics increase their chances of quitting successfully if they check into a rehabilitation centre. A problem at work can be solved quicker if you retreat to planning conference where 100 percent focus is on the issue. Isolate the problem and you have a much better chance at solving it.

- Chip away at the problem. The best time to work on a problem is before it happens. The next best time is as soon as you realize there is a problem. The worst time to work on a problem is after it has grown fangs and a nauseating smell. Immediately begin to chip away at the problem and you will see results.

Problems are meant to be resolved. All do-do magnets be gone.

Love,

Dad

Vince Poscente is a New York Times bestselling author, Speaker Hall of Fame inductee, and Olympian (www.vinceposcente.com). Vince is a husband and father of three who reserves plenty of time for his family; perhaps it is not surprising that a man who delivers much of his keynote from atop a chair would value balance!

Goodnight

Dear Branson, Morgan, and Mitchell,

Tomorrow I fly my first trip since September 11. I would be lying if I said I was comfortable going back to work and being away from each of you. For the first time in my pilot career for United Airlines, I realize that returning home following a trip is not guaranteed.

Tonight, as each of you sleep, this realization fills me with wonder. Have I done my best as a father to share with you thoughts and ideas that will bring meaning to your life should I no longer be in it? Have I whispered to you words of hope and given valuable memories? Have I shared with you some of my most important beliefs in case I don't have the opportunity to share them with you tomorrow? Tonight I am afraid of the answers. . . .

I made a promise to a friend a number of years ago that I would never again stand on the sideline of life watching the game go by as others made their contribution . . . without adding to it some of my own. Tonight, perhaps for the first time, I understand fully the contribution that is mine to make and the legacy it will leave behind. It does not involve fame, fortune, or world enterprise; it involves *each of you*. From this moment forward I honour my promise to a friend and jump fully into what I know to be life's greatest privilege, fatherhood.

Some endeavours are best begun tomorrow, next week, or next year. Not this one. Like viewing your perfect sunset filled with reds, oranges, and blues, other opportunities last only a limited time and must be viewed now before they are lost forever. Eventually, for all of us, the sun will set and take with it our opportunity to share, influence, guide, and touch. Tonight you must know that each of you provide the colours comprising my perfect sunset. I will let the sun drop no further without sharing more of myself with you.

Each of you will discover in life a handful of people that bring to you their life-changing voice of value. These people are truly the gardeners of the soul and their voice needs to be cherished. One of those voices in my life, and the friend to whom I made a promise years ago, was Jason Dahl. His voice was silenced on 9/11 as the captain of Flight 93 when his aircraft was hijacked by terrorists and crashed in a baron Pennsylvania field. Jason was a colleague, a mentor, an inspiration, and a friend. It has been over two weeks since 9/11. I cry most every day and I miss him.

Jason's constant challenge to me, and the one I pass on to each of you tonight, was one of personal contribution. On 9/11 Jason provided gentle encouragement to me one more time, not by words spoken but by observing his family and his life lived. Jason's contributions were many. His most important contribution, however, and the one that will ensure his legacy, was the gift he gave as a father and is best illustrated by his son Matthew's eulogy last week.

"My father never, ever, missed a chance to read with me," Matthew said. "Every night he was home we would lay in bed together and read stories. We would spend time together talking, reading, and laughing. I have brought along our favourite story, and, if it is all right with all of you, I would like to read it, just one more time, for him."

He read *Dr. Seuss's Sleep Book* cover to cover. The first few pages he was able to change his voice so that if you closed your eyes, just for a moment, it sounded like Jason's voice reading. Finally emotions took over and Matthew reached the end of the book. After a long pause staring down at the closed book, Matthew looked up and finished his eulogy. "Goodnight Dad."

Tonight I commit to making a better contribution to each of you every day, a father's contribution, by sharing with you words that have brought me meaning, books that have brought me motivation, places that have inspired me, and ideas delivered from those who have touched me most. Tonight I would like to share with you words and ideas inspired by my friend Jason Dahl.

Each of you has a unique gift and talent to share with the world. It is a gift that only you can give. When found, nurtured, and shared with those around you, your gift will change the world. The moment you commit to discovering and utilizing your gifts and talents an incredible life journey will begin for you. Abraham Maslow said it best, "A musician must make music, an artist must paint, a poet must write, if he is to be ultimately at peace with himself. What a man can be, he must be." Tonight I invite each of you to understand it is never too early to begin thinking about what it is that you must be and never too late in life to find it. Pursue what is in you with every ounce of your being.

As you begin to seek out this seed of potential, know that no far away shore needs to be visited and no exotic destination sought. Your gifts lay not with others or alongside any material thing but wait inside you. It is there you must search and there you will find that the potential for you and for your life is without limit.

If there was only one seed I could share that would begin for you the miracle process it would be this: share your incredible gift with the world. It is not enough to simply find your gift — you must share it with others and understand your contribution will make a difference for those around you. The world and all in it are waiting for your contribution. It is your contribution that will create a legacy and make the world a better place as a result of you having lived in it. There is no other reason for your time here. The answer to life's toughest questions will always appear when you learn to first help others.

I would never have been able to predict the tragedy of 9/11 or the loss of a close friend. I also understand that tragedy and adversity are part of life. While I struggle to deal with the days and months ahead, I will remember that adversity is part of the learning process and many times carries with it unseen gifts of its own. While I am not sure of the reasons behind 9/11, I am positive that what can appear to be your worst moments in life is sometimes just an invitation to yourself and to your next magical journey — a journey you would never have had the courage to take unless forced to do so. As I move forward I will search for this next magical journey. The only gift presented from this tragedy may be the reminder of the importance of fatherhood. If so, it is enough and it is a blessing.

Daddy leaves on a trip tomorrow. If, for some reason, I don't return I would like to share with you words (from Richard Bach) included in my eulogy for Jason: "Don't be dismayed at good-byes. A farewell is necessary before you can meet again. And meeting again, after moments or lifetimes, is certain for those who are friends."

To be with me again, anytime in your life, is simple. Look inside yourself to find your gifts and talents. Use your unique gifts and leave the safety of the sideline and instead jump fully into the game of life with both feet and start helping those around you. Make a difference. Make sure the world is a better place for you having lived in it. It is in this game you will find me, waiting for you. It is in this sacred place you will find me smiling at you, cheering for you, and waiting to hold you again. Know tonight it has been my life's greatest fulfillment having you as my children. Most importantly, know that we are friends and we will be together again, forever.

I love each of you more than I can put into words.

Good night.

Dad

Mark Hoog is a commercial airline pilot. He lost a very special friend and mentor during the terrorist attack of 9/11. He was so kind to share this letter to his children with us. Reprinted with permission from Mark Hoog. Copyright 2006.

Give to Get

Shale, Jacqueline, and Sabrina,

If you looked in the bottle, you would find two key messages: Invest in Yourself, and Give to Get.

A financial advisor will tell you that a great retirement requires you to invest early and invest often. As teenagers, retirement is certainly not top of mind. But the concept of investing early and often is a key message if you're investing in yourself.

What kind of investments can you make? The obvious ones are those that you make in your mind and body: get a great education and make sure you keep fit. But there are other ones, too: develop a love for music, the arts, and relationships with others. The greater your investment, the greater your return. These are activities that you can enjoy throughout your life and make you a far more interesting person.

My second message, Give to Get, follows naturally. The more you contribute to your community, the more you will be enriched by it. The more you help others, the more others will want to help you. Give to Get can make the world a far better place.

You may think that these two concepts are in conflict. Invest in Yourself is all about you, while Give to Get is all about others. In one sense this is true, yet the most successful and happy people have recognized that success and happiness come only with Balance.

Dad

Randall Craig is the author of six books on Social Media and Networking. He can be reached at @RandallCraig and www.RandallCraig.com.

À toi l'enfant que j'aurai

Allô toi, mon petit «zygote» d'amour!

Je ne te connais pas et je t'aime déjà. Si tu savais depuis combien de temps que je t'attends et je rêve à toi. Il m'a fallu d'abord rencontrer ta maman. Il y en a très peu comme elle. En fait, elle est vraiment extraordinaire. Tu vas voir, tu vas vraiment l'adorer. Je crois qu'une des choses les plus importantes qu'un père puisse faire pour son enfant est d'aimer sa mère et crois-moi, j'aime beaucoup ta maman.

Je ne te connais pas et je t'aime déjà. Seras-tu un garçon ou une fille mon petit «zygote» ? Qu'importe, je t'aimerai de tout mon cœur. J'ai hâte de te serrer dans mes bras et de sentir ton odeur de bébé. J'ai hâte de te faire boire et te donner ton bain alors que tu joueras avec tes petits canards jaunes dans l'eau et que tu me feras de grands sourires avec les quelques dents que tu auras dans la bouche. J'ai hâte de te bercer en te racontant de belles histoires afin de t'endormir le soir. J'ai hâte de t'aider à faire tes premiers pas. J'ai hâte d'aller jouer à la balle avec toi dans le parc. J'ai hâte de t'acheter ta première paire de patins.... . J'ai tout simplement hâte de t'apprendre la vie.

Je ne te connais pas et je t'aime déjà. Sache que je serai toujours là pour toi, dans les bons et les moins bons moments. J'applaudirai tes réalisations et j'essuierai tes larmes lorsque ta peine sera trop grande. Je serai là pour t'encourager dans tes rêves les plus fous car j'estime que le plus beau cadeau qu'on puisse donner à son enfant est de l'élever en lui faisant sentir qu'il peut accomplir tous ses rêves.

Je ne te connais pas et je t'aime déjà. Je m'efforcerai d'être un exemple à tes yeux car je crois qu'un enfant a besoin davantage de modèles que de critiques. J'aimerais te transmettre les valeurs qui me sont chères et qui t'aideront à faire de toi une personne autonome, responsable et épanouie. Des valeurs comme la passion, l'équilibre, la volonté, le respect, la responsabilité, la discipline, le travail, le plaisir, l'amitié et l'amour.

Je ne te connais pas et je t'aime déjà. Je ne pouvais pas m'imaginer passer ma vie sans te connaître. Il me manquait toi pour être complet et accomplir ma mission sur terre. Tu seras la lumière dans mes yeux, la chaleur dans mon cœur et le gardien de mon âme.

Mais plus que tout, je promets de t'aimer car je crois que mon rôle de père n'est pas seulement de te donner la vie et de pourvoir à tes besoins physiologiques, ce serait trop facile, mon rôle de père sera avant tout de te donner de l'amour.

J'attends avec impatience ta venue dans notre monde merveilleux et rempli de possibilités qu'il me fera grand plaisir de te faire découvrir. Je ne te connais pas et je t'aime déjà.

Ton papa

Patrick Leroux CSP est conférencier professionnel et auteur de huit livres sur la motivation et les stratégies de succès. Vous pouvez le rejoindre au 1-888-993-8882 et vous inscrire gratuitement à son bulletin du succès en cliquant sur www.patrickleroux.com.

2:12:32 p.m.

Dear Asaf,

On Wednesday, March 5, 2003, five high school students left their school, Ort "Chana Senesh" in Haifa after yet another school day. The group included three girls and two boys. They walked toward the nearby bus station. Their objective was to catch Bus 37, which would have taken them home. When they approached the station they saw two number 37 buses.

The first bus was packed with school students from the nearby "Wizo" school who had been dismissed earlier than usual. Instead of getting on the bus with the Wizo students, the group approached the second bus. One of the boys stepped into the bus and saw someone he had fought with recently who he did not want to encounter that day.

He turned around and stepped off the bus. "I will take another bus," he said to the group and went off, leaving the rest of his group on this bus. The girls on the bus debated where to stop for lunch. They considered two places and finally chose the Carmel Center. They started to go off the bus but before doing so, they asked Asaf, the second boy in the group, if he wanted to join them.

Asaf replied that he was tired and was going home to rest. Ortal, Asaf's girlfriend, kissed him goodbye and he promised to call her later as she departed with the other girls in the group. While on the bus, Asaf called his friend Daniel and asked him what was planned for later; they chatted for a minute and Asaf promised to call later. Just another normal casual teenager call.

A few minutes later and after passing two more bus stops, at 2:12:32 p.m., the bus exploded. The explosion was heard all over the Carmel area.

Asaf, you were almost seventeen years old and you were killed on spot.

104

It's only after you died that I suddenly recognized there are so many things I wanted to do with you, tell you. It's now that I understand that I will never see you grow up, never see you get married or be a father yourself.

I have learned not to take my children for granted, to live life as if it's the last day of your life, and not to leave things undone or unsaid. I enjoy the time with them, give them the freedom to grow up enjoying their time on the face of the earth, life is not a race, and we control not only our own but also our children's lives.

There's nothing that I can compare to losing you, the pain is unbearable and the nights of trying to recall how you looked the last time I saw you, the hours of trying to imagine how you would be looking today, these are agonizing.

The light and happiness of our lives today comes from our remaining boys Arik, Almog, and Eitan. They keep us alive and we need to return as much love as possible to them for that and for being with us.

Love,

Yossi

Yossi Blondi lost his son Asaf to a suicide bomber on March 5, 2003, at 2:12:32 p.m. Yossi remembers his son through various campaigns. Visit his site and help him create an everlasting message at www.blondi.co.il.

Am I a Cool Dad?

Dear Rebecca and Mark,

I would start off by saying you are two great kids, and I give a lot of the credit for this to your mom. That being said, I assume I have had some influence — hopefully positive.

I have always wondered whether you considered me a cool dad. I guess time will tell. In my view, the real test is whether you like hanging out with me and are not embarrassed when I am around. I think I pass this test for now, so then I ask why.

I know it's not because of the way I dress. I am constantly advised of my fashion faux pas.

You very seldom ask me for advice, so I know you do not consider me a teenage sounding board. However, I do offer unsolicited advice on a regular basis, whether you want it or not!

I have come to the conclusion that you hang out with me because of the way I behave. While you often call me a nerd, tool, idiot, and so forth, you at least say this with a smile on your face.

I am a firm believer that in life you need to lead by example. I will not expect you to do something that I would not do myself. Here are some examples of things that I hope you will accept as important role modelling from me:

- Life is too short not to enjoy it; therefore, keep smiling.
- I very seldom swear.
- I exercise a lot.
- I am a competitive person. While winning is not everything, you must be personally satisfied that you did your best.
- I think education is important.

The list can go on and on. You know that "what they see is what they get."

In addition, your family should always come first and they need to know this. It is hard to imagine, when someone is working between fifty and sixty hours a week that their family comes first. The key here is to make sure you are there to show support for your kids. If you do not attend their activities, help them with homework or encourage them to always improve; they would probably think you do not care. I sometimes go overboard on the "encourage to improve" part, but to me that is a father's job.

At the end of the day, regardless of whether or not I'm a cool dad, I hope you know I love you and support you.

Love,

Dad

Gary Gaudry is president of Maritime Travel in Nova Scotia, Canada. Gary is an avid athlete and consummate professional. He and Julie have been blessed with two wonderful children and love to explore the world together.

Just in Case

Dear Haley and Nicole,

If you are reading this it is because I am with God in heaven. If your mom passed on along with me, then we are together now and forever. The last thing in the world I would have ever wanted to do is leave both of you and your mom. However, sometimes things happen that don't seem fair at the time, but ultimately we see that we have become better people because of it. My hope is that you each will deal with this passing in a way that will make you better women, wives, and human beings.

I'm convinced that none of us is meant to go through life without facing serious loss and disappointments. That doesn't mean that life is harsh or unfair. I believe that God allows us to face these challenges so that we can learn to grow. Don't ever use my death as an excuse for not achieving everything that you want to achieve. That would break my heart. Don't grieve too long. We want you to be happy, to get on with your lives and have your hearts filled with joy. You both have such love, compassion, and family support that you can and will realize any dream you set for yourselves.

Both of you are gifted. By that I mean you come from parents who have hopefully instilled in you either by example or heredity the values of hard work, patience, persistence, belief in yourselves, a positive outlook, and self-discipline. What you achieve in life certainly has a little to do with luck: you happen to be born in the greatest nation in the world to a family that loves you and thinks that you are the most important people on the planet. Beyond these blessings, however, you create the vast majority of your own circumstances in life. You have a responsibility to yourselves to create the life you want to live. No one else can do this for you. And there are no excuses. When we make excuses for abandoning our goals and dreams we are only fooling ourselves. I know far too many people who have gone through life always making excuses for why they couldn't stick with a goal. In the end they had a life of excuses. And life is so wonderful and fulfilling when you work towards your dreams.

It is not in the fulfilling of dreams that we achieve contentment; it is in the striving. I believe we are not put on the planet just to have fun. We were put here to live meaningful lives. Of course we should have fun, take time off, and relax. And do a lot of laughing. But these things are not our primary goals; they are just there to help us recover from the efforts of pursuing our larger dreams. Your goals of course are going to be unique for each of you. That being said, there are several little pieces of advice that a father is allowed to give to his daughters as they grow up. Depending on how old you are when you read this, you'll either hopefully remember that we set a good example for these principles or talked to you about them. If not, here are Dad's tips for you, Nicole and Haley, for living a meaningful life.

Your health: Take care of yourselves physically. Do a sport, activity, or exercise to keep you in shape and make you feel good about yourself. Remember, the lousiest workout in the world that you do is ten times better that the perfect workout that you don't do. Speaking of perfectionism, both your mom and I have that trait in abundance. It is a weakness we both struggle with. As our kids, you may have it as well. Keep in mind perfectionism will too often be an excuse for not doing anything because it won't be done perfectly. This isn't good. In my wiser moments — they are rare but happen now and then — I live by a practice that I encourage you to embrace, "Implement now. Perfect later." That applies to exercise as well as to the rest of life.

Your education: Be a lifelong learner. You don't have to decide exactly what you want to do for the rest of your life when you are eighteen. But don't take the easy route and quit school right after high school for a year or two to "find yourself" and figure out what life is supposed to hand to you. That creates a loss of the momentum that you'll need at that critical stage in life. At eighteen, you are smart enough to know some general direction that you wish to pursue and probably have a good idea of what kind of life you want to have for yourself. Don't worry so much about the particular career you'll have as you do about the kind of life you want to be leading. Select a broad enough area of study to give you some options for the future. Then get on with your formal education.

Please don't dabble in your education. Just because it's paid for, don't take one or two courses per term while you take it easy and party with friends. Make a commitment and work hard to achieve it. Understand it's not just the education you're developing; it's the self-discipline, time management, and self-respect. That's a big part of your education.

Your career: You do what you darned well decide is what you want to do for a living. Don't let the rest of the family or friends or society dictate what you will do for work or where you will do it. If you want to weave baskets in Guatemala, then make it happen. A lot of people who don't have the same courage will discourage you (not anyone in the family — they will be a huge support). But others won't see your dream as clearly as you do. Life is short. My only dream for you is that you'll pursue yours with dogged persistence. But this has to be *your* dream.

Your relationships: Ask your mother. Kidding! Wish I had some advice on being a good spouse. I don't really have any beyond the obvious — love and respect each other and learn when to shut up. By that I mean just because our ego thinks of something selfish or unkind that we feel we should say, it doesn't mean it needs to come out of our mouths. More important perhaps than figuring out how you and your husband are going to get along — I hope it's a husband and not some other version of a "life partner," but I guess if that did happen your family would learn to accept it and of course still love you — I think the critical question is to decide who is going to be your husband. By far the smartest thing I ever did in life was ask your mom to marry me. That wasn't just a fluke. After having too many relationships that didn't work, I finally literally sat down and wrote a list of all the qualities I wanted in another person. These weren't just a wish list of good qualities; these were qualities that I needed in order for another person to get along with me — and my flaws. They included the person's outlook on family, health, children, religion, money, career, communication, sex — the whole thing. Then I assigned numbers as to which things were more important than others. Finally, I took every person I'd ever dated and scored them as to how much of a fit they were for me. And of course, who was at the very top of the list by a huge margin? Lydia Mae Grassl, later Lydia Mowatt and your mom. That's the smartest thing (and the greatest bit of persuasion) I've ever done. Maybe give it a shot, especially if you are simply "in love." That's infatuation. Been there. Doesn't work. True love is much deeper and involves a shared vision of day-to-day living — and it does work.

The only other piece of advice I have about relationships is the importance of integrity. Your reputation with others will be based largely on two things: 1. how you treat others (even when they aren't in the room), and 2. living up to your commitments. One little expression I've tried to live by is, "Make promises sparingly. Then keep them — no matter what it costs you." Do that consistently and you'll develop a great reputation. Opportunities and relationships will come your way. Life will be good.

Your finances: This is a blessing and a curse. If both your mom and I have died, then that means you've got a good-sized inheritance. The blessing is that we have provided enough for your upbringing, education, and a start in life. It would be a curse if, knowing you have a trust fund due to you, you decided to take the easy route, not bother with your education and squander the money. That would ruin your life; it would diminish your development of character. That's not what the funds are meant for. We don't mean for you to not have to work or to merely use the money to travel the world and buy toys. Don't do it. If I sound like an annoying father, it's because that's part of my job. That being said, once you get an education and are pursuing your career, please do use the funds to give you a start. It's a gift that we are proud to give to both of you.

Beyond all this Haley and Nicole, I hope that you'll enjoy the blessings of life in this beautiful world. Learn how to be self-reliant. That means enjoying your own company. Take care of yourself: take a self-defence course. I would never expect you to stick with it for as long as I did (although that wouldn't be a bad thing). But I would like you to know how to defend yourselves, even by taking a few lessons and staying fit. Learn how to change a tire, how to cook for yourself, how to manage happily on your own. Then get out there and meet other people. By the age of twenty-five (at the latest) you should be living on your own (perhaps rooming together, but no longer living like children with guardians). I encourage you both to travel, see the world. (First get your education, and then reward yourself with an extended trip.) Experience other languages and cultures. The Turks say that when you learn another language you gain a soul. Read lots. Get out into nature and into the world. It's scary travelling and meeting new people. And it's worth it.

Last piece of advice: take care of each other. You will at times disagree with how your sister thinks, feels, and what she believes. That's her business. You are each entitled to think, believe, or feel any way you want to. That applies to your views on religion, politics, or anything. However, you are each fully responsible and accountable for the things you do and say. You can agree to disagree on differences of opinion. When it comes to how you treat yourself and others, I want you both to watch out for and watch over each other for the rest of your lives. Hold each other accountable to do the right thing. And stick by each other. You may not always be best friends and that's okay, but you'll always be the only ones left of this immediate family. Work out your differences. Learn when to shut up. And learn when a true friend says something to a person who really needs it.

And another thing; I know, I said that last bit of advice would be it. But hey, this is my last chance to be a nagging dad.

Indulge me. Honour the guardians we've chosen for you. We chose these people out of all the people on the planet. They love you and we think they are great role models for you. We will always be your only parents, but they are your family. You are to listen to them and live by their rules. If we didn't agree with their judgment wholeheartedly we wouldn't have chosen them for this most important (and fun) role — raising Nicole Leigh and Haley Elizabeth Mowatt.

The greatest joy in my life has been being a father to the two of you. I once heard the difference between pleasure and joy. Pleasure is catching a fish. Joy is watching your child catch a fish. I wish I could have been here longer to be physically present with each of you as you catch life's fishes; although, it would have been impossible to be in two places at once to see both of you at the same time. This way I'll be watching both of you wherever you are. That's my greatest dream come true for me. My hope for you is that you, in turn, will achieve your dreams. I love you and will be with you for the rest of your lives. God and I will be listening to you. Till we meet again.

With all my love and kisses, always,

Dad

Jeff Mowatt (www.jeffmowatt.com) is an expert in customer service. Living in Alberta, Canada, Jeff creates a global impact in the art of customer service through his message of "influence with ease." Jeff is a proud father, adoring husband, and a centred individual.

Editor's Note: When I first spoke to Jeff about the idea for Message in a Bottle *he told me he already had a letter written for his girls, which he wants them to receive after he has passed away - and this is his letter. Jeff is always ready for anything! I am continually in awe of his selfless willingness to give.*

The Little Porcelain Plaque

To my dear children, Valérie and Jean-Nicolas,

When I was born, my uncle gave a little plaque to my father to hang on the wall of our house. A little white porcelain plaque printed with Gothic style letters, a gold trim, and a few lines of wisdom written in Italian. It followed us to every home, even making it safely to Canada when we immigrated to this country.

For some reason, the older I got, the more the plaque intrigued me. The day that I realized the message was written in a foreign language, I asked my father to translate it for me:

What Children Think

At the age of three: Dad knows everything.

At the age of eight: Dad knows almost everything.

At the age of twelve: There are many things Dad doesn't know.

At the age of fifteen: Dad doesn't understand anything.

At the age of twenty: I might ask Dad for his advice.

At the age of forty: If I only still had Dad.

Every few years, I would glance at the ages on the Plaque and compare the words with my perception of my own dad, sometimes agreeing, sometimes disagreeing with what was written. However, the day that my father was diagnosed with terminal cancer, the last line of those words of wisdom took on a very special meaning. It was the only line I would see every time I visited him. As the months went by, I knew the countdown for those final words had begun. On the fourth day of April 2007 he passed away.

When I went back to his house to pick up the plaque, instead of feeling sad, I realized that I was very lucky. My father had outlived the last prediction. In my mind it will forever read, "At the age of 48: If I only still had Dad."

As you can see, no one can predict fate. No one can change it. But life is nonetheless an amazing journey to be cherished every step of the way to the last line of the plaque.

It is now my turn to hang the plaque in our house so the story can go on.

With all my love,

Daddy

Nabil Doss is known as "the French voice of Paramount Pictures in Canada." Nabil is an experienced narrator whose voice talent is behind many corporate names and events.

Marriage Can Be a Bed of Roses

Dave,

I just read your email announcing plans to marry Karma. If you've both thought it out and both of you truly believe you love each other strongly enough to last a lifetime, then God bless you guys!

Marriage isn't always a bed of roses; that is very true, but I never for one moment regretted marrying your mom. My life would be quite empty without her in it. She is the angel God sent to me when I was convinced I'd never marry again. Some questioned our marriage back then: I am fourteen years older than your mom, we have different backgrounds, different religions, different everything, but our mutual respect and love is the same. I know we will love each other even after our lives have ended. I will continue to write poems for and about her the rest of my life.

So I wish the two of you the same kind of true love, one based on trust, honesty, respect, and concern. Laugh together always! We do it and find it really works.

Your mom and I send you and Karma our love.

Sal

Salvatore Buttaci has been writing since childhood, he has enjoyed seeing in print his poems, short stories, articles, and letters in publications here and abroad. Sal's writing has appeared in the *New York Times*, *USA Today*, *Cats Magazine*, the *Writer*, to name a few. He lives in Princeton, West Virginia, with Sharon, the love of his life.

Make Your Mark

Dear Rosalie and Isabelle,

When we are little we believe that our parents are all-knowing, all-seeing people without faults. As we get older, however, in our years of rebellion we realize the truth that parents are ultimately human and make mistakes, give bad advice, and use the ever seeing you bit as a way to make sure you stay in line.

Often times during these rebellious years, we cease to believe much of what our parents have told us as we feel a bit betrayed. This is normal. Later on, when we have children of our own, we come to realize as we assume the power of being a parent that many of the words of wisdom our own parents passed down are actually true.

My only concern in all of this is that along the way what I consider to be the most important lessons in life may be lost or forgotten while you go through these transitional phases, or that as the world changes (as it always does) your view of these important tenets of life will be watered down in favour of just going with the flow, becoming like many in the world today who become self-absorbed.

So I will in this very brief letter try to remind you of those few things I hope you will never lose. Let me also say that even as young as you both are now, I am so very proud that you exhibit the knowledge of these already, and I hope that no matter what changes we go through, your connection with these life lessons are not a thread that binds you only to me but they are what will connect you as people to the rest of the world. The love I feel for you both will never break the ties that bind us.

Life can be viewed as a road that goes on forever; we create goals for ourselves and they appear in the distance. Sometimes they appear close enough to touch but remain just out of our grasp and it can get very frustrating. Take solace in the pride you ultimately feel in the work you exert trying to attain these goals, as this is as much of a reward and sometimes more so than the actual goal itself.

We ultimately learn the most from our struggles and failures in life and these are what create our values, beliefs, and feelings of self-worth. Do not settle for less than you want out of life but do not keep score; just keep trying.

Take great pride in hard work and never measure your success or failure on your ability to get everything that you want every time you attempt to get it. As you travel this road of life your path will always cross the paths of others; some will travel this road with you for a long time and some will be with you for a brief time.

Regardless, discover who these people are, what they think, how they feel; find your connection with them and be ready if it is something you feel is a worthy cause to invest your time and energy in bringing about change. Resist the temptation to say I will leave these things to others as that is the easiest path; ultimately, it leads us down the road to apathy.

Be active in your community and never become so self-absorbed that you forget you are one of many souls that inhabit this planet. Vote, march, coach, teach, write, lead, and follow. These are but a few of the things you need to do to be active in the world around you.

However, never expect thanks in return for your effort; do it because it is the right thing to do and because it needs to be done by you. Ultimately, we are all judged in this world not by how far we have travelled but by the mark we have left on the landscape and the impressions that we leave on those who have crossed our path.

Leave your mark on the world and pass that on to your children as I have tried to pass mine on to you.

I love you.

Dad

Tony Panza is a third-generation steelworker married to Ermelinda. He is active as a coach, union activist, as well as in his community. He remembers all those who left their mark on him.

A Letter from the Front

Stationed on the front lines of life at the University of Massachusetts Dartmouth, I was already well into my sophomore year of college before realizing I knew absolutely nothing about the opposite sex.

I'd just met Tonia Brightman. Although friends and family predicted she would be just another in my long line of conquests, Tonia had different plans. In one way or another, she'd lit a fire in this roaming bachelor's heart and to everyone's shock, I dove headfirst into her flames.

On an immediate and desperate quest for understanding, I wrote home for reinforcements:

> Dear Dad,
>
> As always, I hope this letter finds you and Mom well. Things are good here at school and I have no doubt that English Literature is the perfect major for me. So, relax! Your investment is being well-spent.
>
> Dad, forgive me for cutting to the chase, but I need help. I think I've finally met "THE ONE!" Her name is Tonia. She's beautiful and sexy, with dark hair and eyes to match, but the problem is she's confusing the hell out of me.
>
> Every time I think I know how to act, I'm wrong. Every time I think I've reacted correctly, I'm wrong. I wouldn't ask if it didn't mean so much to me. I really do need your advice!
>
> Love,
>
> *Steve*

I still imagine that my father dropped the letter onto the end table, leaned back in his rocking chair, and placed both hands behind his head. With a mischievous smile, he undoubtedly pondered my quest into the unknown. Half of him probably felt bad, while the other half must have chuckled.

Women could be a rough trip for sure, but my dad always joked that there was no better ride on earth. He responded with love:

Dearest Steve,

First and foremost, your Mom and I are well and I'm happy to find you are the same. Also, you should know no matter which path you choose, you'll always be a solid investment.

With that said onto the pressing matter at hand. Steve, above all things, you MUST be yourself, both in action and reaction. If any relationship demands differently, then it is destined to fail anyway. So, be you!

The rest is not as simple, so bear with your old man and let's see if I can't shed some light on your wonderful dilemma. By the grace of your lovely mother, I have learned: women are creatures of the heart, not intended to be understood, just loved.

Mysterious by their very nature, they reveal only what they wish, leaving the rest to the efforts of those who dare to explore them within. They live by their feelings, rely on their instincts, and wonder why their needs are not understood without their ever explaining them. But trust me Steve, there has never been a more beautiful creature made by the hand of God.

Intentionally or subconsciously, women will test your heart and constantly check its depth. They can easily detect wandering eyes or sniff out anything less than the truth without even being in your presence. They only wish to be placed first, though they will never request it.

They desire solid communication, but will rarely say it. And they only yearn for someone who will understand them completely, though they will never, ever show their entire hand.

But what a wasted life, my boy, to never know their ways. All women are maternal and protective, almost territorial, when it comes to those they love. They can break your spirit with a look, or heal your soul with those same eyes. There is no softer touch, nor destructive hands, depending on the circumstance.

The truth is found more in what they don't say than in what they will have you hear. And little things like flowers and poetry mean more to them than you could ever imagine. Possessing such complexity, it is still the simple things that seem to make them smile. But oh, the incredible joys you can reap in return.

These beautiful creatures like to feel the safety provided by a man, though they will fight to retain their independence. They are compassionate and sensitive, and though they desire the same from a mate, they are also attracted to the crude ruggedness accompanied by raw masculinity.

I suppose mysterious is not the word. Steve, as I sit here and write this letter, it has become comically clear to me that I know so very little on the subject you ask. So, it looks like the rest becomes your research project. Trust me, son, if Tonia is "The One," your assignment will last no less than a lifetime.

Love always,

Dad

PS When and if you do find some answers, let me know. I've always been just as curious!

Steve Manchester is the father of three beautiful children. Steven Manchester is the published author of *The Rockin' Chair*, *The Unexpected Storm*, *A Father's Love*, and *Jacob Evans*, as well as several books under the pseudonym Steven Herberts. Three of his screenplays have been produced as films. See www.StevenManchester.com

Keep Up the Good Life

Dear Jordin and Lindsay,

Now that you have ventured out into the working/married world, I have been reflecting on the "messages" you would have received from your mother and I throughout your youth that hopefully will stand you in good stead as adults.

I always thought our role was to teach you to evaluate risks and be safe, not to be overprotective. While both of you have experienced a number of injuries during your play, these adversities are an important part of growing up.

Challenging yourself to perfect that skateboard trick, ski double black diamonds, or jump higher fences on your horse have inherent risks. Not to challenge is an even bigger risk. Keep striving!

We tried to create a climate in which you felt comfortable engaging in activities that interested you. This meant that while you dabbled in organized sport, you found your real pleasure and reward in spontaneous play, usually involving skis, skateboards, horses, outdoor rinks, and of course music. Keep playing!

I was overjoyed when you saw that your education was far bigger than formal schooling. You have learned a lot through your experiences/apprenticeships that took place throughout Canada, and I was glad to have played a role in nurturing that philosophy. Keep experiencing!

I hold dear the many thoughts I have of your generosity toward and caring for others. You have learned that people, particularly friends, are very much at the heart of our existence and spontaneous acts of kindness affect everyone they touch in a positive way. Keep giving!

In many ways you saw us as role models. You didn't try to become exactly like us but rather took what we said and did as tenets that you used to build your own personalities and characters. Keep growing!

Even though you live in Springhill and Vancouver now, we continue as a family to love, laugh, and cherish the memories together, particularly at Christmas. Keep loving! As a family we have learned a lot together over the years.

Keep up the good life!

Love,

Dad

Ted Scrutton is an avid outdoor enthusiast who invested his professional career in ensuring that people could enjoy the wilderness. He has raised two beautiful children and feels blessed to see their continued success.

I'm So Proud of You

Dear Mackenzie and Kennedy,

Your first day of school for the year, grade three and grade one; I can't believe how quickly the two of you are growing up. To see you both running around the house this morning, so excited to start a new school year, brought a huge smile to my face.

I can't believe how fast the last two months have gone by and I want you to know that I had a great summer with you. It was a blast swimming in the lake, riding our bikes to the store, going to the beach, and hanging out doing fun things.

It's truly a beautiful thing to see you both growing into smart, independent young ladies, even though a part of me would like to see you stay the pretty little girls you are today.

As I look back on the summer and the days since you were born, I am grateful for all the time and memories we have shared. You both mean the world to me and I am so proud of you both.

I love you both with all of my heart,

Dad

xoxoxo

> Trevor Sinclair is a financial advisor for CIBC Wood Gundy. He and the love of his life, Jackie, are enriched by the love of their community and their two most precious gifts, Mackenzie and Kennedy.

Wander

Dear Emery and William,

Indulge your father for a few moments while I tell you the story of a trip your mother and I once took, as there are several lessons at the end for you to consider.

A few years ago we flew to Marrakesh, intending to spend a few days there and then fly across Morocco to Fez. But something happened in that gorgeous city, which seems eternally soaked in late-afternoon light.

Essentially, your mother had a brainstorm, which happens fairly often when we travel and which you will one day learn to anticipate, and possibly even enjoy, though this may take many years.

Her idea? Ditch our flight to Fez travel instead to the Sahara Desert in the southern part of Morocco, and get there in time to ride a camel out into the desert and watch the sun rise.

We argued. Rather, I argued.

A crazy idea, I said. How will we get there? Where will we stay? Why change our perfectly good plans now? As you surely know by now, your mother can be quite persuasive.

In short, we decided to change our plans. Rather than board a plane, we hired a driver to take us across the Atlas Mountains and into the desert. We saw Berber villages cut into the sides of mountain peaks; we saw ancient sand-and-mud towns rising out of the barren desert; we saw verdant gorges cut from the mountains over the centuries by roaring rivers.

After a fourteen-hour drive we arrived at an oasis and a tiny inn run by an expat Frenchman, who served us wine and cheese he'd bought earlier that week in Algiers. Sometime after midnight, after writing about the day in our journal, I left your sleeping mother and walked out to the spring for a swim.

I was alone in an ice-cold oasis under a full moon in the desert. The night was completely black and completely silent, the moon so enormous I thought I could reach up and touch it. It was one of the most memorable moments of my life — the kind of moment when you are conscious, even while you are still having the experience, of the fact that you will remember it forever.

The knock on our door (no phones, naturally) came long before dawn. We were driven by SUV further out into the desert, until we came upon a Berber camp. We each chose a camel and mounted (your mother still likes to imitate the groan my camel made when he tried to stand with me aboard), and were led over increasingly higher dunes toward the east.

Finally, on the highest mound, we sat and watched the most beautiful sky you can imagine, watched the first light hit the dunes in front of us, watched the colours deepen and shift in the sky and over the sands. And it was the second time in the space of a few hours that I had one of the most memorable moments of my life.

So why do I tell you this story now?

Here's why: because it sums up some of the most important lessons that your mother has taught me and that I, in turn, hope to teach you.

First: make plans, but don't be afraid to alter them or reject them altogether. When new information appears or if changed circumstances warrant, be willing to adapt and to try something unexpected.

Second: once you decide to strike out in a new or unexpected direction, don't regret the path not taken — throw yourself into the course you've chosen and enjoy and appreciate it as best you can.

Third (and perhaps most important): wander. I wish the two of you many happy journeys throughout your lives.

Your father

Tim Brandhorst is a writer, editor, and publisher. He lives in Chicago, Illinois, with his wife, Amy, and their twins Emery and William.

Twelve Years Old: To My Son Borden

My dear son,

How dear you are to me you will never know, or how hard it is for me to leave you, perhaps never to return. You can never understand unless you go through the same ordeal yourself someday, and I hope you may never have to. But if you do, face it boy, face it bravely, do not back down. I love you with all the power of love within me and now, on the eve of my departure for war, I am writing you. And if I do not come back, this will help you to understand why I went, why I took such a risk, why it was necessary. I am a man and being a man I could not stand by and see our country in danger and not do my best to save it. It does not appeal to all alike. If you grow older you will realize more fully what I mean. Perhaps when you read this, the war will be over and there will be peace in the world once more.

It may be my lot to fall and not return with the troops, and if so, I would like you to always remember that I loved you better than life itself. I have looked forward to the time when you would be a little older and I would be helping you shape your future and giving you a father's counsel and you would have the benefit of the years of experience I have had. We would be good friends you and I, the best of friends, you are my oldest son, and I hope you will grow up to be as good a man as you promise to at present, my boy. Always be good to your mother; if my actions deprive you of a father, you will still have one of the best mothers. You cannot afford to neglect her honour; and love her above all else and you can safely rely on her counsel and judgement. Be kind and true to Grandma, she is Daddy's mother and has a great store of wisdom for boys and girls.

I must think of you as a boy of twelve, a big boy, a true boy who will make a man. True men are not plenty and all boys are not true boys; be a true boy. There are things to be true to, first be true to your "God." Second, be true to yourself. Third, be true to your country.

You can be true to your God by obeying His commands, carrying out His will, and being kind to all His greatness.

You can be true to yourself by treating yourself fairly. God has given you a body to go through this life, use your body in the way He would wish you to. Keep your body clean, that will keep it healthy; keep your mind clean by reading good books, thinking good thoughts, and doing kind acts. Choose clean friends and always be friendly. Never go back on a friend, one good friend is worth a great many poor ones. In your play and daily contact with your friends and school fellows be clean in your conduct with them, particularly with the girls; remember you are a gentleman and treat them as ladies. No matter what they are like, it will not excuse you; avoid the bad ones, you cannot afford to spend time with them — that would not be treating yourself fairly. To get an education, God has given you a time of youth to prepare your mind, knowledge gained every day, but only one day at a time.

You will get tired of school and you will see boys who do not go very much and you will think they get along just as well. But they will not, and they will perhaps find it out in time. Study your lessons each day, one day at a time, and you will find the better you know your lessons the better you will like to go to school. You will not be true to yourself unless you learn your lessons each day as they come along. You are storing up knowledge that will be most useful by and by. Get your storehouse, "your mind," stored with the useful knowledge you get at school and as you go through life you will always find use for it. No man can take it from you and you cannot lose it; you will always have it.

Be true to yourself in your play. Play fair or not at all. A boy who will not play fair is likely to make a man who will cheat in his business; they are both on the same road, although the business comes a little further along. You can be true to your country by being a good citizen, ever ready to defend what is right and oppose what is wrong. As you grow to manhood you will have to decide on many questions, "public questions," and take one

130

side or the other. It is your duty to do that, decide honestly and then act accordingly. If filling any office of any society, or in any public capacity, do your best. This is all included in "citizenship" of the right kind. It is not always necessary to die for your country, to serve her; you can live for her, only do your duty as you see it and you will be fulfilling your obligations.

And now my own dear boy may God keep you, protect you, and watch over you and make you worthy of the love bestowed upon you. Be kind to your sisters. You have two sisters now and I hope you will have them for many years. You and Douglas love each other, which is right. I know you both love your sisters and they love you. How happy you will be.

My own dear boy I must close. I cannot express my love for you. Again, may God keep you and watch over you.

Your loving father,

J. H. Tupper

Submitted by Peter Davison from a letter written to his grandfather Rev. Dr. Borden Tupper in 1916. Major J. H. Tupper never returned to Canada. He was killed in the Battle of the Somme during World War I.

Words in a Bottle

Dear Seth and Jessica,

When I was a child, I never anticipated the joy I would receive from having my own children. My early days were a simple Saskatchewan prairie life like W. O. Mitchell's *Who Has Seen the Wind*. When you were born I wished for you to have the same idyllic early years I encountered while laying in the tall grass watching cloud formations change above the prairie wheat fields.

How can I fill a bottle of wisdom for you when we each make up our own way into the future? It is very simple: we are part of a universal rhythm handed down through our family generations and indeed long before, throughout the history of the earth. Once you find the groove you will know it; however, if you have moments of struggle keep searching because life has a way of teaching us if you lose your way.

What keynotes of wisdom can I send to you?

1. The history of the earth is 4.5 billion years; if we are lucky we live for a hundred years. In the grand scheme, it's not a long time so make every day count.

2. Do work you love and you won't work a day in your life.

3. Find your passion and work with joy towards achieving a life filled with mitzvot (doing good deeds).

PS . . . I am very proud of you and your accomplishments. . .

All my love,

Dad

Growing up in Mitchellton, Saskatchewan, and Calgary, Alberta, Ken Allan Drabinsky developed a passion for earth sciences and music which first manifested in a successful rock band. Ken's company says it all: Geospirit Consulting, mapping "in the spirit of the earth." Ken is married to the gifted Natashia Halikowski.

Dad's Advice

Dear Natashia, Dianne, and Jim,

Here are some thoughts I have found to work well and I hope will guide you well:

1. Be the first to say you are sorry; there is always another point view . . . so think before you speak. Remember, the last word in any argument is rarely the best.

2. Always be willing to be of service. Always give a minimum 60 percent, hence my 60:40 formula and my principle to guide you: give more than you expect in return.

3. My advice for success with others is to follow the golden rule: do unto others as you would have them do unto you. Be free with the respect and the kindness you give to others and they will give back the same.

4. Don't look back . . . it can stop you. Look ahead and you can go anywhere. Do anything one step at a time and keep your eye on where you want to be.

5. You can always bounce back from failure. You can always learn, you can always improve, and you can always change.

6. Take responsibility for what happens and ask yourself these questions: "What did YOU do to create this? Now what can you do to change this? When is the time to get on with it?"

Love,

Dad

Hal was born in Manitoba in 1924. He joined the Navy as a seaman in 1942 and served overseas in the Royal Canadian Naval Volunteer Reserve on the HMCS *Summerside*. He transferred to the permanent Navy in 1945 and served in the Korean War. Hal served his country for a total of forty-four years with Department of National Defence.

Postscript: Hal passed away in March 2010 of asbestos cancer. Apparently the Destroyers of the time used asbestos and Dad, along with many courageous sailors, suffered the same fate. He is survived by his wife Ellen and his three children. Hal was a gentle, kind man who was always there to lend a hand and always a man with deep principles. We remember Dad best when we raise a glass and share his favourite toast — "Happy Days."

Different Meaning of Family

Kylee, Aimee, and Natalee,

It seems like only yesterday when each of you were born, and as I write this letter, you all have grown so much. I want to tell you how much you mean to me and what you mean to me. Being adopted has meant that I grew up without knowing my biological family. I was blessed with having two wonderful parents who "chose" me as their own. That said, you girls hold a deep connection with me, and you are the only biological family I know and have.

Kylee, you are my oldest, which means I have known you the longest. There are so many memories already in such a short time. I remember the day you were born... I remember my Captain at the firehouse, a big, tall, deep-voiced man who kicked my bed at 6:00 a.m. and said, "It's time." At the hospital, I was so anxious and excited to meet you. I was trying to be funny, so the nurses were going to lock me up in the closet, or so they said. It was all in good fun.

I also remember the story you love to tell people, where I had just fed you your bottle, was lifting you up, and you threw up all over me. You love telling people that I had my mouth open, too.

You also love telling people about the one time I went to the firehouse with my toenails painted after a makeover by you and your sisters.

I know you are still too young to understand this, but you are setting the pathway for your sisters. They look up to you and want to do the same things you do. Be patient, be proud, and respect your sisters.

Aimee, my middle child, I remember the scare we had during the time you were in your mother's belly. Gratefully, everything was fine and the world is blessed with your presence. I remember at the hospital, the doctors and nurses were shocked at how much water your mother had when the doctor broke her water.

You are probably going to be the shortest of the three. Sorry about that. Blame your mother. I love waking you up every morning, as I hear you fire off your "gun." Sometimes it's so loud, it shakes the bed. A girl should not be able to fart that loud.

And your laugh, I will never forget your laugh. I can recognize that laugh anywhere. Keep on laughing. You are a warm and caring person. Your friends and family mean so much to you and I see how important they are to you. Don't ever change.

Natalee, my baby, it seems like you were born only yesterday, and yet here you are, almost starting school. I remember cutting your umbilical cord, just like I did with your two older sisters. I also remember you had a knot in your umbilical cord, just like Kylee. They called it a "true" knot. They say it is lucky, and I am lucky to have you as my daughter.

I remember when you could first walk, and how you would go up to any man and just grab his hand and walk away. I am sure you would have walked away with them, if I didn't stop you.

Everyone knows you for your long hair and how much you hate it being brushed. Hence I had to learn how to braid hair and my attempts at French braiding are improving. You, too, have a laugh that always brings a smile to my face.

I also love the fact that when I am trying to discipline one of your sisters, you are always the first one to point out that you listen to me, or that you were a good girl.

Being a professional firefighter has blessed me with another type of family, my brothers and sisters in the fire service. People think that, as firefighters, we are big and strong, yet we bleed and breathe just like everyone else. During my shift, there are times when we might get on each other's nerves, or someone is just being a pain or even just having a bad day: kind of like the way you three get along sometimes. But when the time calls for it, I can always count on my brothers and sisters at the firehouse, just like you guys can count on me and each other.

I have seen a lot of people at their worst, and when times are sad and dark, I feel so lucky to have you girls. All I do is think of you, and it cheers me up and puts a smile on my face. I carry you close with me every day at work, as your pictures are in my helmet.

I am sorry that your mother and I are not together anymore. It doesn't mean that we love you any less; it just means that sometimes mommies and daddies grow apart. The great thing for you is that you get two Christmases, two birthdays, two bedrooms, etc. . . . and in a way, you now have two families. Just like me.

Girls, I just want to say that I love you to the moon and back, around the world and to the airport and back (stolen from Natalee). Please grow up slow, enjoy being a kid, and respect and love your friends and family.

Daddy loves you.

xoxoxoxo

Jamie Graven is a single dad with shared custody of his three daughters. When he is not on duty as an engaged dad with his girls he is on duty as a lieutenant with the Halifax Fire Service improving the lives of his community.

Guess Who's Pregnant?

Dear Emily,

When I found out Mommy was pregnant with you, our lives changed in the most powerful ways. We were driving into town from the cottage and she said, "Guess Who's Pregnant?" I rhymed off a big list of people in our lives, she kept saying, "No." Finally I looked over at her, frustrated I couldn't guess, and when I saw your mommy's eyes and her little smirk I INSTANTLY knew that Mommy was pregnant. I couldn't see through my tears of joy, so we had to pull over and just let them all out.

When you were born, the nurses cleaned you up, wrapped you up, and then placed you in my arms. When your head touched my arm emJ, it was the most profound moment of my life. It was a surge of energy that I've never felt before and I can guarantee can NEVER EVER be duplicated. So it goes without saying that you are absolutely one of a kind, sweetheart.

I want to share with you FIVE very important reminders.

YOUR LIFE MATTERS

Above all else, know that you matter, you have value, and what you have to say and do can impact this world in a powerful and positive way.

BE as Opposed to DO

Doing is important. Taking action is key, but it's important to stay rooted in where your action comes from. Deciding and working on WHO YOU WANT TO BE will determine your success no matter what you end up doing. If you say, "I want to BE someone who is compassionate," then the action comes from those roots. BE amazing emJ.

Get Back Up

You will fall down in life. The real challenge for me will be to let you fall down. But, remember, whenever you fall down, YOU GET BACK UP.

LEADERSHIP IS IMPORTANT, BUT NEVER BE AFRAID TO BE A PLUS ONE.

One person can make a difference. YOU CAN make a difference. BUT actual change happens not with the power of one, but with the power of one plus one. You can never do anything alone. Sometimes leadership is supporting someone else and joining in!

Volunteer

Your life matters, and once you see this deeply, you see that EVERY LIFE IS IMPORTANT, including the lives of animals. Continue to shine with compassion and remember that other people need our help. Continue to be giving with your skills, time, and funds.

Love,

Dad

> Philly D or "Phil Doucette" is a passionate human being. He is a professional speaker, author, yogi, and loving husband and father. He and his wife Ryann own several Moksha Yoga studios. Phil lives by a simple mission statement, "To live with the understanding that there are no ordinary moments." Visit him at www.phillyd.com.

Thank You for the Journey

To my dearest sons,

The pride and joy of having children is something that you can never explain to anyone. Only a parent who goes through it can fully appreciate it. To look at a child and see a small human being that comes from you is an amazing experience and brings a lump to your throat. However, parenting does not come with a manual that ensures you are successful. Although there is more information available these days, very little is provided to prepare you for the years that lay before you.

Having children goes in stages. The early years have a long-term effect on the child even though the child does not remember those years. The next phase is the period of maturing from infancy to children and early teens. Some of this is remembered and this is where the relationship really starts its journey. The next phase is the late teens and early adulthood — probably the most difficult for both parties as the relationship is put under the most pressure. Next is adulthood until the parent starts to age and this stage can depend on how successful the previous stage was. Finally there is the age where the parent ages and this can be a more challenging stage for totally different reasons.

I was not good at the infancy to teens or teens to early adulthood (although I was a bit better the second time around). I tell you this so that you can appreciate and understand these stages when your turn comes. I wish someone had explained to me that there were stages and what it meant at each stage. I did not have the luxury of having great parents as role models for me, and so that made it even more confusing.

I believe that the hardest bit of this journey was going from telling you what to do (infancy) to helping you to make up your own mind (teens) and finally to leaving you to make up your mind knowing that my role was simply to catch you when you fell over. It is the hardest part because parents want their children to learn from their mistakes and not make the same mistakes they did when they were kids. In reality, we all need to make our own mistakes, but that is hard for a parent.

So as we enter the phase when I age, I know this will challenge us both in a new way. The role reverses and I struggle to not be like my father was to me. We will survive because at the end of the day, we love each other more deeply than we often cared to show.

Thank you for the journey, and I hope you enjoy your journey as much as I have enjoyed sharing my journey with you. Never doubt one single thing: I always love you. . . .

Love,

Dad

Paul Bridle is a leading edge consultant, speaker, and executive leadership coach. He operates a consulting business that helps organizations to be more successful in the global marketplace. He has two wonderful sons and the best wife a man could wish to share his life with. Visit him at www.paulbridle.com.

First Practice Gratitude

My sweet girls,

You will never know how amazing it has been to be your papa and to watch you grow. This life is a gift bigger than we could ever imagine. It can also be a little confusing at times, so here are some things I have learned that I feel have guided me through my days on this planet.

First off, practice gratitude. It is so important in this world that we see and feel how lucky we are to observe and participate in the unfolding of the universe. To think that over the course of 13.5 billion years, a collection of carbon molecules have come together to make up your body is amazing! And to see what else has evolved over this period of time — the trees, the animals, the mountains, the rise and fall of nations, and the masterful inventions of curious minds — it is all a miracle. I say "practice" gratitude because there will be times when you don't feel grateful, and it will be good to have this practice to fall back on. To be grateful even when things appear terrible and unfair and hurtful — that is a skill and an art form, and I wish for you mastery of that art.

Which leads to openness. I would love for you to stay open to hurt, confusion, and betrayal. Life is so interesting in that it is never easy to find happiness at all times. Nor would I want that for you. The sweetness of joy and the ecstasy of love come from the contrast they provide to the pain and hurt that we experience as we grow. Strangely, my every cell wants to protect you from hurt and pain, yet I am also aware that it will happen as you grow. So stay strong in those times, and remember that there are lessons to be learned when we bump up against the sharp things that life presents. We learn how to be graceful, generous, and forgiving simply because we can relate to and accept our pain.

As such, I hope that you will always consider the impact that you have on the world around you and the earth itself. Don't let anyone ever tell you that your contributions to the world don't make a difference. Every piece of litter that you dispose of properly makes the world cleaner, every kindness that you offer to others ripples out to people you will never meet, and every dollar that you ever spend will go towards either making the world more fair and equitable, or less so. You are powerful, and your thoughts and actions matter, so be kind to people, animals, and the earth. I promise you that you will make a difference.

On that note, I would like you to know that the ultimate contribution that you can make to the world is to help create peace. Not everyone sees how their actions affect the planet or others, and so I hope that you can counter that by cultivating peace in your own heart and mind. This takes some hard work, and so I am hopeful that you will make efforts towards peace, whether through meditation, yoga, prayer, service/social activism, or study. If human beings were ever to have a reason for being on this planet, it would be to leave it as balanced, peaceful, and pristine as it was when we came into the world, if not more.

Beyond and within all of that, be curious, creative, adventurous, and humble. Take chances, and strive to see things as unique and part of all things at the same time. This will allow you to be more connected to others and leave you more open to understanding your place in the world. This is called humility, and it is your ticket to being fully absorbed in this wonderful journey through life.

Love,

Dad

Ted Grand is the Director and Founder of Moksha Yoga Inc (www.mokshayoga.ca), which has studios across North America. He lives with his family in Ganges, British Columbia, where he continues to live and grow daily in a peaceful and caring way.

Keep Your Vision Clear

Dear Chris, Jenn, and Vanessa,

There's an exponentially expanding abundance of electronic/ print resources and advice to living a happy and successful life. But as a lifelong personal growth and leadership student, I can easily point to visioning or imagery as the core principle from which all others emanate, like ripples of water growing out from the centre.

Visioning is where my personal effectiveness quest began. In 1974, when I was just starting my commission Culligan sales job, someone recommended I read Claude Bristol's book, *TNT: The Power Within You*. This book sparked such intensity of energy, excitement, and profound new awareness that I couldn't get a good night's sleep for almost a week. Even now, as I thumb through the book and recall that turning point in my life, a shiver runs up my spine.

Published in 1954, this was Claude Bristol's second book. His first, which I read later, was *The Magic of Believing*. Both books were based on his decades of searching for a deeper understanding of and applying what he called "mind stuff." This work came from his experience as a journalist, studying and reporting on the full spectrum of spiritual and religious movements (especially fringe groups), building his own wealth and career as an investment banker, and his study of thousands of books on "the science of thought."

Here are just a few of the many key passages and ideas from *TNT* that started my self-leadership juices flowing (the emphasis shown is his):

"Picture the force! It is the explosive force of a mental picture of what you want in life, given by you to your subconscious, touched off by faith in yourself and faith in God. Whatever you picture, within reason, can come true in your life if you have sufficient faith in the power within! That's your TNT — a mental picture of what you want and the faith that you can and will get it . . . we do not think in words. We think in pictures!"

"The universal language is feeling . . . this creative power operates like a magnet. Give it a strong, clear picture of what you want and this creative power starts to work magnetizing conditions about you — attracting to you the things, resources, opportunities, circumstances and even the people you need, to help bring to pass in your outer-life what you have pictured . . . what you picture in your mind, if you picture it clearly and confidently and persistently enough, will eventually come to pass in your life . . . there is a universal law in the mental realm, 'like attracts like.'"

TNT awakened me to the enormous power between my ears that I wasn't using. I began reading many books and magazine articles on these topics and I attended presentations and workshops given by many of the leading authors, trainers, and speakers. I bought dozens of audio tapes on this and related "mental attitude" topics.

A strong early influence was personal development speaker and author Zig Ziglar's audio tapes and book, *See You at the Top*. In his book, he wrote about the importance of "seeing the reaching." He went on to state, "The world has a way, not only of stepping aside for men or women who know where they are going, but it often joins and helps them reach their objective."

Over the next few decades, I used these approaches to build a successful sales and management career, quit smoking and biting my fingernails, to lose weight, get into better physical shape, develop my writing/speaking skills, build two successful training and consulting firms, and help hundreds of thousands of people around the world with "mere words."

Through visioning, I even changed from being a "sickly kid" (I would miss weeks of school each year) to not missing a single workday because of sickness for a period of nearly twenty years. I blew my record with a number of ailments, unprecedented depression, and "sick days" in 1993 when the picture of my career future was the foggiest it had ever been. Once the picture of my preferred future cleared up, so did my attitude and health. Our thoughts become things and really do manifest themselves in our lives.

Whether you think your world is full of richness and opportunity or bleakness and despair — you're right. It's exactly like that — because that's your point of focus. By focusing there, you turn your expectations into reality. What you see for yourself is intertwined with the context of your life. That context attracts the people you associate with, your discipline and habits, and determines your perceptions of "reality."

Visioning creates passion; the clearer and more compelling the vision, the stronger the passion. And the more likely you are to hang in there during the inevitable downs and defeats as you reach for your dreams. Visioning or picturing my preferred future has been my greatest source of energy and focus.

I fervently want to see you have a happy, satisfying, and very successful life. My vision for you has hopefully helped you get a good start. Your vision for yourselves will determine the quality of your journey and where you finish.

Love,

Dad

Jim Clemmer is an expert in practical leadership and personal growth. His company has provided hundreds of thousands of people worldwide with improvements in personal, team, and organizational success. He is the proud father of three beautiful children and lives in Kitchener–Waterloo, Ontario. Join him at www.jimclemmer.com.

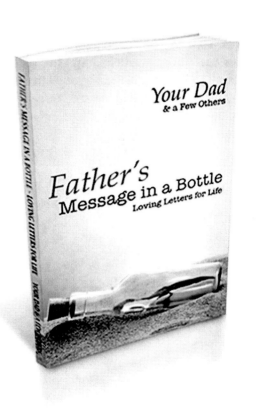

Do you have a letter to share?

If you are interested in getting a letter published in an upcoming "Message in a Bottle" Book — we would love to hear from you!

Our books are written by our expert readers — that means you. So burn up your computers keyboard and fire us off a letter for an upcoming book. We'd love to read your letter, and consider it for an upcoming addition! We are currently welcoming submissions for upcoming titles including:

- Mother's Message in a Bottle
- Grandma's Message in a Bottle
- Grandpa's Message in a Bottle
- Sister's Message in a Bottle
- Brother's Message in a Bottle
- Kid's Message in a Bottle
- New Mother's Message in a Bottle
- New Father's Message in a Bottle

To submit your letter go to www.messageinabottlebook.com and follow the links. Writers are not paid for their letters. However, if we publish your submission, you will receive a first run edition of the book that your letter appears in. It is a small token of thanks for sharing your loving letter for life.

Hope to read your letter soon.

Tyler

Message in a Bottle Book Series

www.messageinabottlebook.com

CPSIA information can be obtained at www.ICGtesting.com
Printed in the USA
LVOW040204200412

278357LV00006B/4/P